Taxation of Canadians in America

Dale Walters, CPA, PFS, CFP®
with Sally Taylor, CPA, and David Levine, CA, CPA

Self-Counsel Press
(a division of)
International Self-Counsel Press Ltd.
USA   Canada

Self-Counsel Press acknowledges the financial support of the Government of Canada through the Book Publishing Industry Development Program (BPIDP) for our publishing activities.

Printed in Canada.

First edition: 2013

Library and Archives Canada Cataloguing in Publication

Walters, Dale, 1958–
Taxation of Canadians in America / Dale Walters.

ISBN 978-1-77040-133-4

1. Canadians—United States—Finance, Personal.
2. Canadians—Taxation—Law and legislation—United States.
3. Canadians—Legal status, law, etc.—United States.
4. Canadians—Retirement—United States.
5. Income tax—Law and legislation—United States. I. Title

HG179.W35 2012   332.024008911073   C2011-908403-1

Self-Counsel Press
(a division of)
International Self-Counsel Press Ltd.

Bellingham, WA   North Vancouver, BC
USA   Canada

Contents

Introduction   xiii

1 The Basics of US Taxation   1

   1. History of the Internal Revenue Service (IRS)   1

   2. The Basics   3

   3. Dealing with the IRS   4

   4. The IRS Examination (Audit) Process   6

   5. Filing   8

      5.1 When to file your Individual Income Tax Return
(Form 1040)   10

      5.2 Electronic filing   11

      5.3 Penalties and interest for underpayment,
late filing, and late payment   11

      5.4 Filing status   12

   6. Notifying the IRS about Your Change of Address   13

2 Your First Year in the US   14

1. Determining US Residency   14

    1.1 First year elections   17

2. How Do I Get an Identification Number?   20

3 The Treaty   23

1. Residency   27

2. Real Property   29

3. Dividends, Interest, and Royalties   30

4. Gains   31

5. Personal Services   32

6. Artists and Athletes   33

7. Pensions and Annuities   34

8. Social Security   35

9. Government Service   36

10. Students   36

11. Taxes Imposed by Reason of Death   36

4 Canadian Taxation of Nonresidents   38

1. Who Is Considered a Nonresident of Canada?   39

2. Selling Property in Canada   45

5 Foreign Tax Credits   47

1. What Are Foreign Tax Credits?   48

2. Types of Foreign Income   51

3. How to Calculate the Foreign Tax Credit   52

4. Alternative Minimum Tax (AMT)   55

6 Registered Retirement Plans, Pensions, and Social Security   57

1. Registered Retirement Plans   58

    1.1. Deferral   58

    1.2 Distributions   59

	1.3	Planning	61
	1.4	How the taxes work	66
	1.5	Other types of accounts	70
2.	Pensions		71
3.	Social Security		72
	3.1	The Windfall Elimination Provision	73

7 Investments — 74

1.	Securities Law			74
2.	Mutual Funds			75
	2.1	Passive foreign investment company (PFIC) rules		76
		2.1a	Qualified electing fund (QEF)	77
		2.1b	Mark-to-market election	78
		2.1c	Excess distribution	78
3.	Tax Reporting Slips			79
4.	Taxation of Specific Types of Investments			80
	4.1	Municipal bonds		80
	4.2	Government bonds		80
	4.3	Annuities		81
	4.4	Personal residence		81
	4.5	Investment real estate		81
5.	Treaty Rules That Affect Your Securities			82

8 Common Deductions — 84

1.	Above-the-Line Deductions	85
2.	Trade or Business Expenses	86
3.	Vacation or Rental Home Expenses	87
4.	Depreciation, Amortization, and Depletion Expenses	91
5.	Individual Losses to Property	92
6.	Alimony and Child Support	94
7.	Contributions to Individual Retirement Accounts (IRAs)	94
8.	Moving Expenses	96
9.	Health Savings Accounts (HSA)	96

10. Qualified Education Expenses and
    Student Loan Interest   97

11. Exemptions   98

12. Standard Deductions or Itemized Deductions   99

    12.1 Standard deductions   99

    12.2 Itemized deductions   100

13. State and Local Taxes   101

14. Interest Expenses   101

15. Medical Expenses   103

16. Employee Educational Expenses   105

17. Charitable Contributions   106

18. Miscellaneous Itemized Deductions   108

19. Credits   109

    19.1 Child and dependent credit   110

    19.2 Credit for the elderly or disabled   110

    19.3 Child tax credit   111

    19.4 Earned income credit   111

    19.5 Education credits   111

    19.6 Retirement savings contributions credit   112

    19.7 Other credits   112

9 Tax Planning   114

1. Tax Planning in General   116

2. Specific Tax-Planning Opportunities   117

    2.1 Your principal residence   117

    2.2 Other real estate investments   118

    2.3 Securities   118

    2.4 Series EE bonds and I bonds   119

3. Tax Breaks for Senior Citizens   119

4. State Income taxes   119

5. Community Property   121

10 US Estate and Gift Taxes

		123
1.	US Nonresident Estate Tax	127
2.	US Resident, Noncitizen Estate Tax	131
2.1	Jointly held property	135
3.	Gift Taxes	135
4.	Generation Skipping Transfer Tax	137
5.	State Estate and Inheritance Tax	138

11 Leaving the US

		141
1.	Expatriation	142
1.1	Your rights after renunciation of US citizenship	148
1.2	The Reed Amendment	149
2.	Tax Planning before You Leave	150

Conclusion

151

Resources

153

About the Authors

157

Tables

1	Income Threshold for Filing	10
2	US Immigration Options	21
3	Your Status: Nonresident Alien or Resident Alien	22
4	Treaty Articles	26
5	Types of Income and Withholding Rates	37
6	RRIF Minimum Withdrawals by Age	63
7	Summary of Expenses	76
8	The Format of the US Individual Income Tax Return (Form 1040)	85
9	Trade or Business Expenses	88
10	Vacation/Rental Home	91
11	Classes of Depreciation Property	92
12	Standard Deduction Amounts	99
13	Additional Deduction Amounts	99

14 Limits on Medical Deductions   105
15 Gift and Estate Tax Rate Schedule   132
16 Unified Tax Credits and Exclusion Amounts   133
17 State Estate and Inheritance Tax   138

Notice to Readers

Laws are constantly changing. Every effort is made to keep this publication as current as possible. However, the authors, the publisher, and the vendor of this book make no representations or warranties regarding the outcome or the use to which the information in this book is put and are not assuming any liability for any claims, losses, or damages arising out of the use of this book. The reader should not rely on the authors or the publisher of this book for any professional advice. Please be sure that you have the most recent edition

Prices, commissions, fees, and other costs mentioned in the text or shown in examples in this book may not reflect real costs where you live. Inflation and other factors, including geography, can cause the costs you might encounter to be much higher or even much lower than those we show. The dollar amounts shown are simply intended as representative examples.

Circular 230 Disclaimer: Nothing in this book is to be used or relied upon by anyone for the purposes of avoiding penalties that may be imposed on you under the Internal Revenue Code of 1986, as amended. Any statements contained within this book relating to any federal tax transactions or matter may not be used by any person to support the promotion or marketing to recommend any federal tax transaction. Everyone should seek advice based on their particular circumstances from an independent cross-border tax advisor. No one, without the express written permission, may use any part of this book in promoting, marketing, or recommending an arrangement relating to any federal tax matter to anyone else.

Acknowledgments

Robert (Bob) Keats, was the first person to see a need for US-Canada financial planning, and has been serving Canadians and Americans with US-Canada cross border issues for more than 30 years. In 1990, he founded Keats, Connelly and Associates, which is now called KeatsConnelly. It is because of Bob's foresight and hard work that we are now able to write the first and only book dedicated solely to the taxation of Canadians in the US.

We also want to acknowledge all of the KeatsConnelly employees, past and present, on their contribution to this book. We have tried to capture their cumulative knowledge in the following pages. Though we wrote the book, it is the cumulative effort of decades of employees learning this subject matter by working directly with clients day-after-day, year-after-year, that we have been able to accumulate the knowledge we are putting into this book.

Ultimately, if it were not for the support and understanding of our spouses we would not have been able to accomplish a large undertaking such as this. Because the time we spent researching, writing, and editing took away time from our families, their patience and encouragement to finish the book was essential.

Lastly, we want to thank all of the clients we have worked with over the years. It is our clients that have put us in a position to be able to write a book on this important topic, and without them this book would not have been possible. It is for our current and future clients that we wrote this book.

Introduction

We estimate that more than 1 million Canadians file tax returns in the US and another 1 million should be filing, but don't. Based on our experience, many of those that do file have a number of mistakes that could be very costly if the Internal Revenue Service (IRS) were to discover those mistakes. Of those who don't file, but should, we find the main reason is that they do not fully understand the US residency requirements and therefore the requirement to file US tax returns.

As Canadians, you can hardly be blamed for the fact that, as a group, your US tax returns are most likely being done incorrectly. Taxation in general is complex enough, add to that rules that are seldom used by most tax preparers, then toss in the Treaty that can modify the Canadian *Income Tax Act* and the US Internal Revenue Code and you have a very complex set of rules. If that were not bad enough, in a number of cases, there are no clear rules or regulations addressing the issues you are facing, which makes it very difficult to file correctly even if you are trying to do the right thing.

This book will attempt to address most of the US tax- and estate-planning issues you will face as a Canadian living in the US. We will be primarily addressing individual taxation because it is the area most people need help. Besides, to discuss the cross-border implications of corporations, partnerships, trusts, etc., would require at least one whole book dedicated to nothing but the tax issues cross-border businesses face. While we will discuss these various entities from time-to-time, we will only cover the issues from the perspective of how they affect you as the individual.

KeatsConnelly is the largest and most experienced cross-border wealth management firm in North America that specializes in helping Canadians and Americans realize their dreams of a cross-border lifestyle. KeatsConnelly was started in 1990 and has more than 35 employees, with offices in Phoenix, Arizona; Boynton Beach, Florida; and Calgary, Alberta.

Cross Border Tax & Accounting is a wholly owned subsidiary of KeatsConnelly that specializes in tax planning and preparation for Canadian and US citizens, who live, work, or conduct business across the US-Canada border. A team of Canadian Chartered Accountants and US Certified Public Accountants prepare all types of US and Canadian tax returns. It is the cumulative expertise and experience of the professionals at KeatsConnelly and Cross Border Tax & Accounting that we draw upon in writing this book.

From our vantage point, the need for cross-border specialists is apparent, but we understand that you do not have our vantage point, so we will try to explain why it is so important to hire professionals that are experts in US-Canada tax planning and preparation.

Here are some reasons that a professional who specializes in US-Canada tax should be used:

- **Prevent risk:** There are risks that are unique to preparation of returns with international issues, such as forms that need to be filed and elections that need to be made. Failure to file a required form can be devastating, literally costing you tens of thousands or hundreds of thousands of dollars. That may not be the worst of it; you could be deported or even imprisoned.

- **It is complex:** Some of the complexities that arise on a regular basis are immigration, deemed disposition of property, residency issues, income, estate and gift taxes, how to title and own assets, the myriad of foreign reporting forms and the related issues and penalties involved, currency exchange, qualifying for Social Security benefits, special elections that need to be made, etc. We contend that it is impossible for someone who dabbles in this area to know all of the complexities involved. We have specialized in US-Canada taxes for more than 20 years and find it difficult at times to keep up with all of the changes going on in this area; there is no way that anyone who is new to this subject should be attempting to prepare these returns.

- **Complexities need to be coordinated:** Immigration should not be undertaken until the income and estate consequences have been considered and proper planning has been taken. You need to consider what actions need to be taken to show the authorities that you are a resident of one country or the other. You need to consider what actions need to be taken before you exit Canada and what actions should be taken after you are a resident of the US. Many of these actions need to be done in a particular order, so you have to know what comes first, second, third, etc.

Here is an analogy for you to consider. If you were building a house, would you go out and hire an architect, a carpenter, a mason, electrician, and painter and not coordinate them? What would happen if the framer did his or her work before the architect developed the plans? What would happen if the carpet was installed before the drywall was hung? We can all agree that the job would be a complete disaster, yet this is exactly what people typically do when looking to move across the border; very first thing they do is hire an immigration attorney to get them a visa. Guess what, you are now subject to a bunch of US tax laws and you have done no planning; it is already a mess and you have barely gotten started.

- **The difference between knowledge and experience:** It is one thing to know that A, B, and C need to be done, it is another thing to know the specifics of how to get A, B, and C done. The perfect analogy here is that of graduating university students. Even if they are in fields such as law, accounting, and medicine, we all know that they have no idea what they are doing when they get out of school, yet they have "learned" how to do their jobs in school. The knowledge that is needed is as deep as it is broad, and it takes experience to learn it. Keep in mind that 20 years as a brain surgeon does not qualify you as a heart surgeon, and vice versa. Similarly, 20 years as an accountant does not qualify that accountant as a cross-border tax specialist.

- **Two experts on each side of the border do not equal a cross-border specialist.** On a regular basis we have clients that come to us who have hired the best advisor in Canada and the best advisor in the US only to find out after spending hundreds of thousands of dollars that the professionals' lack of understanding of the other country's laws created a hurdle they could not overcome. Similarly, those specialists do not typically coordinate with other specialists.

The problem from your perspective (the taxpayer), is that you cannot tell the difference between a correctly filed and incorrectly filed tax return. Understandably, you do not know what forms need to be filed, what elections need to be made, or in some cases do not even know what is taxable income and what is not. If you knew those things, you would prepare your own returns.

The solution is a cross-border tax specialist; someone who focuses on US-Canada tax. That person should have access to cross-border planning professionals who can look at all the aspects of a cross-border lifestyle and coordinates those aspects together, just as a general contractor would coordinate all of the aspects of building a house.

We realize that some of you are skeptical and think that we are simply trying to scare you into hiring our firm to prepare your taxes. Well, you are partially correct; we are trying to scare you, but not necessarily into using our services. There are a handful of US tax specialists who will do a fine job in preparing your returns. Though there may be more, we know of about a half-dozen firms in the US that we would trust to prepare your returns properly.

When seeking a competent cross-border tax specialist, we believe it is fair to be curious about the cost of preparing a US tax return with cross-border issues. Of course, we cannot speak for all of our peers, but based on our experience, you can expect to pay approximately $1,000 at the low end, up to $5,000 at the high end, depending on the complexity of your situation. These estimates do not include Canadian returns or business returns. For your first US return, you can expect to pay double, due to the calculations, elections, etc. that need to be made in the first year.

In the more than 20 years KeatsConnelly has been specializing in cross-border issues, we believe that we have seen every situation and have heard every question. We are using that experience as the basis for writing this book. We are writing this book to address most of the tax issues that Canadians need to know while living in the US.

To the best of our knowledge, this is the first and only book dedicated to the topic of taxation of Canadians living in the US and we hope it will become an indispensable guide for Canadians living in the US.

Other books written by the professionals at KeatsConnelly that are part of the Cross-Border Series include, *The Border Guide: A Guide to Living, Working, and Investing across the Border*, *A Canadian's Best Tax Haven: The US*, and *Buying Real Estate in the US: The Concise Guide for Canadians*. You can find these books at www.self-counsel.com/default/personal-finance.html, www.crossborderseries. com, www.crossborderseries.ca, or crossborderseries.net, or www. crossborderbooks.ca.

We are writing another book that will cover the *Taxation of Americans in Canada*. This book should be released in 2013 and will also be on the Self-Counsel Press, crossborderseries.net, and cross-borderbooks.ca websites when ready.

1

The Basics of US Taxation

The US Internal Revenue Code (IRC) is synonymous with the Canadian *Income Tax Act* and is among, if not the most, complex system of taxation in the world. This book will cover a very small segment of the IRC, and even for the IRC sections we do discuss, we will not be going into great detail.

There are two basic points we want to make sure are clear and said up front; the US taxes its citizens and residents on their worldwide income, and that the US tax burden is about one-third less than that of Canada. In this chapter, we will discuss the Internal Revenue Service (IRS), IRS audits, filing requirements, and the basic layout of a US tax return.

1. History of the Internal Revenue Service (IRS)

In 1862, during the US Civil War, President Lincoln and Congress created the position of Commissioner of Internal Revenue and enacted an income tax to pay war expenses. The income tax was repealed ten years later. Congress revived the income tax in 1894, but the Supreme Court ruled it unconstitutional the following year.

In 1913, the 16th Amendment gave Congress the authority to enact an income tax. That same year, the first Form 1040 appeared after

Congress levied a 1 percent tax on net personal incomes of more than $3,000, with 6 percent surtax on incomes of more than $500,000.

In 1918, during World War I, the top rate of the income tax rose to 77 percent to help finance the war effort. It dropped sharply in the postwar years, down to 24 percent in 1929, and rose again during the Depression. During World War II, Congress introduced payroll withholding and quarterly tax payments.

In the 1950s, the agency was reorganized to replace a patronage system with career, professional employees. The Bureau of Internal Revenue's name was changed to the Internal Revenue Service (IRS). The IRS Commissioner and Chief Counsel are selected by the president and confirmed by the Senate.

The IRS *Restructuring and Reform Act* of 1998 prompted the most comprehensive reorganization and modernization of the IRS in nearly half a century. The objective of the act was for the IRS to reorganize itself in a way that would resemble the private sector model of organizing around customers. Few outside of the IRS would say that objective was met.

The IRS is a bureau of the Department of the Treasury and in fiscal year 2010, the IRS collected more than $2.3 trillion in revenue and processed more than 230 million tax returns.

The following mission statement describes the roles of the taxpayers and the IRS:

- In the United States, the Congress passes tax laws and requires taxpayers to comply.

- The taxpayer's role is to understand and meet his or her tax obligations.

- The role of the IRS is to help the large majority of compliant taxpayers with the tax law, while ensuring that the minority who are unwilling to comply pay their fair share.

The IRS is organized to carry out the responsibilities of the Secretary of the Treasury. The Secretary has full authority to administer and enforce the internal revenue laws and has the power to create an agency to enforce these laws. The IRS was created based on this legislative grant.

The Internal Revenue Code provides for the appointment of a Commissioner of Internal Revenue Service to administer and supervise the execution and application of the internal revenue laws.

2. The Basics

Income taxes are based on income and are imposed at the federal level, most state levels, and some local city levels within the US. Each state or city may define taxable income differently; however, most states refer to the federal law for determining taxable income. Common examples of income that may be taxed differently by a state than by the federal government are Social Security income, interest income from US treasury obligations, and pension benefits from that state's governmental workers. Cities typically tax income earned within that city. Cities that impose a separate tax are generally limited to the states of Ohio, Pennsylvania, and New York. In the US, you must file separate returns to the federal, state, and city governments, similar to filing separate Canadian federal and Quebec provincial returns.

In the US, individuals, estates, trusts, and certain corporations are subject to income tax. Partnerships and corporations that make an election to be treated as a small business (known as making an "S election") are not taxed. Partnerships and S corporations are what are called "flow through" entities. This means that the income, expenses, and ultimately the income tax flows through to the individual partners or shareholders. Nonresidents of the US are not allowed to be shareholders of an S Corporation.

Regular corporations (sometimes referred to as "C corporations") are subject to double taxation because the corporation pays tax on the income and when a dividend is paid, the individual pays tax on the dividend. The corporation does not receive a deduction for the dividend and the individual does not receive a credit for tax paid by the corporation.

Federal and many state income tax rates are graduated, meaning that at higher levels of income you pay progressively higher levels of tax. The tax rate that corresponds to your highest level of income is known as your marginal tax rate. For individuals, the income level at which the various tax rates apply, varies by your filing status.

For the 2011 tax year, individuals are subject to federal graduated tax rates from 10 to 35 percent; the 35 percent tax rate applies to taxable income of more than $379,150 for couples filing jointly and single individuals. Also for 2011, corporations are subject to federal graduated rates of tax from 15 to 35 percent; the 35 percent tax rate applies to corporate taxable income of more than $18,333,333. State income tax rates vary from 0 to 11 percent. State and local taxes are generally deductible in computing federal taxable income.

The Federation of Tax Administrators website www.taxadmin. org/fta/rate/ has information on the latest tax rates, surveys, and rankings.

3. Dealing with the IRS

While the IRS is not the demonic organization it is frequently made out to be, it's an organization you do not want to get on the bad side of. Fortunately, staying in the IRS's good graces is relatively easy to do; file your taxes on time and pay the taxes you are legally required to pay.

In the US you are typically not contacted by the IRS unless it wants something such as additional information. Neither ignore nor panic when you receive a letter or notice; instead, we suggest that you contact a professional and have them assist you with the process. Just because the IRS asserts something, does not mean that it is correct.

Do not pay additional amounts of tax without making sure you owe it. Over the years, we have seen many taxpayers pay additional amounts without checking with us or otherwise confirming that the amount being asked for was legitimate. We guess that based on our experience, greater than 50 percent of the notices sent by the IRS asking for additional money are incorrect in part or in whole.

This is what the IRS says about a notice. "If you receive a letter or notice from the IRS, it will explain the reason for the correspondence and provide instructions. Many of these letters and notices can be dealt with simply without having to call or visit an IRS office. The notice you receive covers a very specific issue about your account or tax return. Generally, the IRS will send a notice if it believes you owe additional tax, are due a larger refund, if there is a question about your tax return, or it needs additional information."

Here is a copy of IRS Summertime Tax Tip 2011-22, August 24, 2011.

Every year the Internal Revenue Service sends millions of letters and notices to taxpayers, but that doesn't mean you need to worry. Here are eight things every taxpayer should know about IRS notices — just in case one shows up in your mailbox:

1. *Don't panic. Many of these letters can be dealt with simply and painlessly.*

2. *There are number of reasons the IRS sends notices to taxpayers. The notice may request payment of taxes, notify you of a change to your account, or request additional information. The notice you receive normally covers a very specific issue about your account or tax return.*

3. *Each letter and notice offers specific instructions on what you need to do to satisfy the inquiry.*

4. *If you receive a correction notice, you should review the correspondence and compare it with the information on your return.*

5. *If you agree with the correction to your account, usually no reply is necessary unless a payment is due.*

6. *If you do not agree with the correction the IRS made, it is important that you respond as requested. Write to explain why you disagree. Include any documents and information you wish the IRS to consider, along with the bottom tear-off portion of the notice. Mail the information to the IRS address shown in the lower left part of the notice. Allow at least 30 days for a response.*

7. *Most correspondence can be handled without calling or visiting an IRS office. However, if you have questions, call the telephone number in the upper right corner of the notice. Have a copy of your tax return and the correspondence available when you call.*

8. *It's important that you keep copies of any correspondence with your records.*

For more information about IRS notices and bills, see Publication 594, "The IRS Collection Process." Information about penalties and interest charges are available in Publication 17, "Your Federal Income Tax for Individuals." Both publications are available at www.IRS.gov.

Caution: One thing to point out is that Canadians seem to be much more likely to call Canada Revenue Agency (CRA) or the IRS to ask questions about the law, than Americans. We suggest that you do not call the IRS for advice for a number of reasons. First and most importantly is that the IRS is not bound by the advice the employees provide on the phone. In the best of cases, you are flipping a coin as to whether you will get an answer that is correct. Given that you will have a number of cross-border issues, this will increase the complexity and therefore decreases the likelihood of receiving an answer you can rely on. We hope the following analogy makes the problem clear:

We provide you a hat full of possible answers, 40 percent of them will be correct answers and 60 percent will be incorrect answers. You are to blindly pull one answer from the hat, then bet thousands of dollars on the fact you have one of the correct answers — that is not a bet we would want to take. Also, when talking to the IRS agent, you may either not accurately convey the issue or you may not understand the answer due to the fact that you do not understand the law or the tax lexicon. Lastly, you may inadvertently tell the IRS agent something you should not be telling him or her.

4. The IRS Examination (Audit) Process

The IRS examines (audits) tax returns to verify that the tax reported is correct. Selecting a return for examination does not always suggest that the taxpayer has either made an error or been dishonest. In fact, some examinations result in a refund to the taxpayer or acceptance of the return without change.

The IRS selects returns for examination using a variety of methods, including:

- **Potential participants in abusive tax-avoidance transactions:** Some returns are selected based on information obtained by the IRS through efforts to identify promoters and participants of abusive tax-avoidance transactions. Examples include information received from "John Doe" summonses issued to credit card companies and businesses and participant lists from promoters ordered by the courts to be turned over to the IRS.

- **Computer scoring:** Some returns are selected for examination on the basis of computer scoring, which means computer programs give each return numeric "scores." The Discriminant Function System (DIF) score rates the potential for change, based on past IRS experience with similar returns.

The Unreported Income (UI) DIF score rates the return for the potential of unreported income. IRS personnel screen the highest-scoring returns, selecting some for audit and identifying the items on these returns that are most likely to need review.

- **Information matching:** Some returns are examined because payer reports (i.e., tax slips), such as Forms W-2 from employers or Miscellaneous Income (Form 1099) statements from banks and brokerage firms, do not match the income reported on the tax return.

- **Related examinations:** Returns may be selected for audit when they involve issues or transactions with other taxpayers, such as business partners or investors, whose returns were selected for examination.

- **Other:** Area offices may identify returns for examination in connection with local compliance projects. These projects require higher level management approval and deal with areas such as local compliance initiatives, return preparers, or specific market segments.

An examination may be conducted by mail or through an in-person interview and review of the taxpayer's records. The interview may be at an IRS office (i.e., office audit) or at the taxpayer's home, place of business, or accountant's office (i.e., field audit). Taxpayers may make audio recordings of interviews, provided they give the IRS advance notice. If the time, place, or method that the IRS schedules is not convenient, the taxpayer may request a change, including a change to another IRS office if the taxpayer has moved or business records are there.

The audit notification letter tells which records will be needed. Taxpayers may act on their own behalf or have someone represent or accompany them. If the taxpayer is not present, the representative must have proper written authorization. The auditor will explain the reason for any proposed changes. Most taxpayers agree to the changes and the audits end at that level.

Taxpayers who do not agree with the proposed changes may appeal by having a supervisory conference with the examiner's manager or appeal their case administratively within the IRS, to the US Tax Court, US Claims Court, or local US District Court. If there is no agreement at the closing conference with the examiner or the examiner's manager, the taxpayers have 30 days to consider the proposed adjustments and their next course of action. If the taxpayer does not respond within 30 days, the IRS issues a statutory notice of deficiency, which gives the taxpayer 90 days to file a petition to the Tax Court. The Claims Court and District Court generally do not hear tax cases until after the tax is paid and administrative refund claims have been denied by the IRS. The tax does not have to be paid to appeal within the IRS or to the Tax Court. A case may be further appealed to the US Court of Appeals or to the Supreme Court, if those courts are willing to accept the case.

Note: Do not attempt to handle an IRS audit on your own; hire an experienced and competent tax professional to represent you.

5. Filing

All US citizens and noncitizens of the US that are residents (referred to as resident aliens) are required to file a US tax return if they meet certain income thresholds. To be clear, if you are considered a resident of the US, you are subject to the tax laws of the US, even if you are here illegally. You are a resident alien if you meet one of the following tests:

- Legal Permanent Resident (e.g., Green Card holder).

- You meet a 183-day substantial presence test. This is a two-part test and if you fail the first part of the test, you are generally a US resident, with limited exceptions. If you fail only the second part of the test, you can file Closer Connection Exception Statement for Aliens (Form 8840) to claim a closer connection to a foreign country (Canada) and will not be considered a US resident, assuming that in fact you do have a closer connection to Canada.

  - **Part 1 of the test:** You are physically present in the US at least 183 days during the calendar year. Note that each partial day counts as one day. The only exception is if you are traveling by plane and you simply pass through the US on your way to another foreign destination.

  - **Part 2 of the test:** You are physically present in the US for at least 183 days using the following three-year formula:

    - **Year 1:** Each day counts as one day.

- **Year X-1:** Each three days counts as one day.

- **Year X-2:** Each six days counts as one day.

For example, if you spent 122 days each year, each of the last three years, this is what you would have:

- In 2011, you spent 122 days, times 1/1 = 122 days.

- In 2010, you spent 122 days, times 1/3 = 41 days.

- In 2009, you spent 122 days, times 1/6 = 20 days.

> Total number of days using the formula, equals 183 days and you fail Part 2 of the test and are considered a US resident unless you file Form 8840.

Note: If you arrive in the US on November 1 and leave on March 31, you would have been in the US a total of 121 days. If you did this year in and year out, you would pass the second part of the test most years. Every leap year, you would have stayed in the US 122 days and therefore failed the test and must therefore file Form 8840 to avoid being considered a US resident and subject to tax.

What makes this rule confusing are primarily two things: the fact that the test has two parts, and the fact that immigration has different rules. Remember that being in the US for less than 183 days is only one part of the test, if you are in the US every year for 122 days or more, you have failed part two of the test and must file Form 8840 to show the IRS that you are not a US resident. If you fail the second part of the test and do not file Form 8840, you are a US taxpayer and subject to US tax. In the Introduction, we mentioned that there is an estimated 1 million Canadians in the US that are residents who are not filing returns. It is this group of Canadians that spend four months or more each year in the US and do not file Form 8840 that we are mostly referring to.

There is another set of rules that you need to be concerned about: the immigration rules. These are the rules that the customs agents at the border are concerned with. These rules use a rolling 12-month period instead of the calendar year the IRS uses. For example, if you stay in the US from October 1 through April 1, you would have been in the US 183 consecutive days, yet only be in the US for 92 days in the first year and 91 days in the second year. If you assume no other days in the US in either year, you clearly passed both parts of the residency test for tax purposes, but failed the test for immigration purposes. To make matters worse, the Customs agents are not consistent in their application of the rules. Fortunately, you are typically looking at only being hassled by the Customs agents and nothing serious comes of it, but it does make it confusing for you when you are constantly getting conflicting answers.

If you are a resident or citizen, you still may not have to file a tax return if your income is less than certain thresholds. Table 1 shoes the income thresholds for two categories. (If these categories do not apply to you, you may fall into another category and corresponding threshold.)

Table 1
INCOME THRESHOLDS FOR FILING

Category	You must file if gross income is at least
Single:	
Younger than age 65	$9,500
Age 65 or older	$10,950
Married filing jointly and living together:	
Both spouses younger than age 65	$19,000
One spouse younger than age 65	$20,150
Both spouses age 65 or older	$21,300

Note: The US defines marriage as a man and a woman who are legally married. However, some states and many countries recognize common-law marriage, so the IRS will recognize common-law marriages if that marriage met, and continues to meet the requirements of that jurisdiction; allowing the couple to file jointly.

While some states and many countries recognize same-sex relationships, the IRS will not recognize them and those couples will not be allowed to file a joint return.

5.1 When to file your Individual Income Tax Return (Form 1040)

The normal due date for filing individual income tax returns (Form 1040) is April 15 of the year following the tax year. If this date falls on a weekend, the due date is the Monday following the weekend. You can get an automatic six-month extension of time to file your return by filing Application for Automatic Extension of Time to File

US Individual Income Tax Return (Form 4868) by the due date, typically April 15. By filing this form in a timely fashion, your time to file will be extended to October 15.

An extension provides only an extension of time to file, not pay your taxes. You must calculate and pay any taxes due by April 15 (or the adjusted date) to avoid penalties. If you are required to make estimated (installment) tax payments, you must make those payments even though your return is on extension.

Not all forms that you may need to file have the same due date. Those forms will in turn have their own forms to complete for an extension for that form, and that form only. Not only do some forms have different due dates, some forms do not allow for an extension of time to file. For example, the Annual Information Return of Foreign Trust with a US Owner (Form 3520-A) for reporting foreign trusts is due on March 15; and Application for Automatic Extension of Time To File Certain Business Income Tax, Information, and Other Returns (Form 7004) is required for the six-month extension, which means that the ultimate filing deadline is September 15, not October 15 like most of the rest of your return. Also, Report of Foreign Bank and Financial Accounts (Form TD F 90-22.1) is due June 30 and cannot be extended.

Filing an extension does not increase your chance of being audited. If fact, if you cannot get your tax information to the accountant early in the season, you may want the accountant to file an extension so that the accountant can prepare the return after April 15 when there is less pressure and he or she hasn't been working 12- to 16-hour days for the previous two months!

5.2 Electronic filing

Paid preparers are now required to file all tax returns electronically, when possible. However, some returns have forms or situations that have not yet been approved for electronic filing. When electronically filing, your accountant will require you to sign the US Individual Income Tax Transmittal for IRS *e-file* Return (Form 8453).

5.3 Penalties and interest for underpayment, late filing, and late payment

If it is determined later (by you or the IRS) that the amount of tax owed is greater than the tax paid when the return was filed, there will be interest due on the underpayment of tax. The interest rate can change quarterly, but it is currently 3 percent for underpayments. The interest is compounded daily.

If you file your return late without a reasonable cause, the IRS will impose a penalty of 5 percent per month, with a maximum penalty of 25 percent. If your return is more than 60 days late, the IRS imposes a minimum penalty equal to the lesser of $135 or 100 percent of the tax due. If the failure to file is fraudulent, the monthly penalty is 15 percent, with a maximum penalty of 75 percent.

If you are late in paying your taxes, the penalty is .5 percent per month, with a maximum penalty of 25 percent. This penalty is in addition to the regular interest charge. This penalty may be doubled (to 1 percent) if after repeated requests to pay and a notice of levy, you do not pay.

As mentioned earlier, the IRS allows you to file for an automatic extension of time, giving you until to October 15 to file your return. However, you must still pay the tax by April 15. There is an exception to the late payment penalty if you paid at least 90 percent of the total tax owed by April 15.

If both the late payment and late filing penalties apply, the .5 percent penalty for late payment (but not the 1 percent penalty for continued nonpayment) will offset the penalty for late filing, during the period that the penalties run concurrently.

5.4 Filing status

There are five filing statuses in the US; single, married filing jointly, married filing separately, head of household, and qualifying widow or widower. In Canada, couples file their own separate returns, in the US married couples can, and typically do, file a joint return where both spouses report all of their income and deductions on a single return. Married couples may choose to file separately, but not as singles.

Note: As of this writing, six states recognized same-sex marriages. Marriage licenses are granted by these six states: Connecticut, Iowa, Massachusetts, New Hampshire, New York, and Vermont, plus Washington, DC and Oregon's Coquille and Washington's Suquamish Indian tribes. Common-law marriages are allowed in the following states plus the District of Columbia: Alabama, Colorado,

Iowa, Kansas, Montana, New Hampshire, Oklahoma, Rhode Island, South Carolina, Texas, and Utah. As mentioned previously, the IRS will recognize common-law marriages, and will allow the couple to file as married filing jointly. In addition to the states listed, couples from other countries that recognize common-law marriages, such as Canada, will also be recognized by the IRS.

While it is usually beneficial for married couples to file jointly, there can be circumstances where filing separately might be beneficial. The most common situation in which a couple might consider filing separately is when one spouse has many more deductible expenses than the other spouse, such as medical expenses where the deduction is limited to the amount that exceeds 7.5 percent of income.

For example, assume in this very simplistic example that Jane has income of $100,000 and her husband Bob has income of $30,000. Bob also had $10,000 of medical expenses, whereas Jane had no medical expenses. If Jane and Bob were to file jointly, they would have $130,000 of income and their medical expenses would be limited to $250, the amount above 7.5 percent of $130,000 (130,000 x 7.5% = 9,750). In other words, the first $9,750 would not be deductible. On the other hand, if they filed separately, Bob would be allowed to deduct $7,750, as only $2,250 would not be allowed (30,000 x 7.5% = 2,250).

6. Notifying the IRS about Your Change of Address

The IRS will send all correspondence to your last known address; this includes any claims of refund or deficiency notices. Keeping the IRS up to date on how to contact you is important because your refund may be delayed otherwise. If you owe the IRS money, simply changing your address and not telling the IRS does not help; the IRS can enforce a deficiency even if you never received the notice, as long as the IRS sent it to your last known address.

To update your address, you can call the IRS at 1-800-829-1040 or by filing a Change of Address (Form 8822), or by correcting the address on an IRS correspondence and returning it with the correct information. We recommend filing the form rather than calling since the 800 number above is the general number and you will be on hold for a very long time. When filing Form 8822, we recommend that you send it by registered mail so that you have proof it was sent and received.

2
Your First Year in the US

Your first year in the US will be full of questions about everything from how do I get to where I am going and where can I go to watch a hockey game, to when are US taxes due and what is deductible for US tax purposes? While we can't help you with the first two questions (though if you are ever in one of the cities where we have an office, we would be happy to share a hockey game with you), we will address most of your tax questions in this book. In this chapter, we will address topics such as when you become liable for US taxes, how you get a tax ID number, and identify some of the special rules that apply only in the first year.

1. Determining US Residency

A foreign national is anyone that is not a US citizen. A foreign national is presumed to be a nonresident alien, unless he or she passes one of the following two tests of being a resident alien:

1. Lawful Permanent Resident Alien card (i.e., Green Card)

2. Substantial Presence Test, which means the person must be physically present in the US for at least —

   • 31 days during the current year, and

- a total of 183 days over the last three years where —

  - all of the days in the current year, plus

  - one-third of the days in the preceding year, plus

  - one-sixth of the days in the second preceding year.

There is also the closer connection exception, which means the person can avoid resident alien status if the taxpayer —

- was in the US less than 183 days during the tax year,

- has a tax home in another country,

- holds himself or herself as a resident of that country, and

- files IRS Closer Connection Exception Statement for Aliens (Form 8840).

Form 8840 is designed to gather information so that the IRS can determine where the taxpayer resides. The form asks the following types of questions:

- Where is your family located?

- Where are your automobiles located?

- Where are your automobiles registered?

- Where is your personal belongings (e.g., furniture) located?

- Where are your social, cultural, and religious organizations located?

- Where are the banks with which you conduct your everyday business?

- Where is your driver's license issued?

- Where are you registered to vote?

- From what country did you receive the majority of your income?

If you are a green card holder, you will be taxed as a US citizen in most respects. If you are out of the country when the card is issued, residency begins the moment you enter the US. If you leave the US, but keep your green card, tax liability continues. The simple reason for this is that immigration law and tax laws are not congruent. For example, if you are out of the country without permission for more than six months, the green card can be revoked. However, you continue to be subject to US tax until the green card is turned in.

Many treaties, including the US-Canada treaty, provide that when you are a resident under the laws of both countries, residence is determined under a series of tie-breaking rules determined as follows:

- You are a resident of the country in which you have "a permanent home."

- If you have a permanent home in both or neither of the countries, residence is in the country in which the economic ties are closer (center of vital interest).

- If the center of vital interest cannot be determined, residence is in the country of your "habitual abode."

- If you have a habitual abode in both or neither of the countries, residence is determined by citizenship.

- If all of the foregoing rules fail, the residence is determined by agreement between the "competent authorities" of the two countries.

If you are taking advantage of any treaty benefits, you must attach IRS Treaty-Based Return Position Disclosure Under Section 6114 or 7701(b) (Form 8833) to your return to disclose the treaty position taken.

In nearly all respects, a resident alien is taxed exactly like a US citizen. The exceptions are the year of arrival and the year of exit from the US. In these cases, the resident alien is a dual-status alien. The taxpayer is called a dual-status alien because for part of the year he or she will be a resident of the US and for part of the year the taxpayer will be resident of a foreign country. In these cases, the taxpayer will be required to file what is known as a dual-status income tax return. The following are important things to remember with a dual-status income tax return:

- Only the income earned while a resident in the US will be subject to US tax.

- If married, you must file as married filing separately.

Itemized deductions are limited to the following:

- State and local income taxes

- Gifts to US charities

- Casualty and theft losses

- Miscellaneous deductions

1.1 First year elections

An important first year election is to step up the basis of your assets for US tax purposes. We discuss this in more detail in Chapter 3, but essentially the Treaty says that if you pay a deemed disposition tax upon emigrating from Canada (which you will do in nearly all cases), you can elect to step up the basis in your assets to the fair market value of the assets on the day before you emigrate. The purpose is to have you avoid paying tax in the US, at some point in the future, when you have already paid tax in Canada on the same assets. Any appreciation after your date of emigration from Canada will be subject to tax when sold.

You must make the election on your first US tax return, using Form 8833. Failure to make the election will result in you being liable for tax on the entire gain, not just the post-exit gain, which will result in double tax. This election is not available to US citizens. We recommend that you actually sell any assets that are subject to the deemed disposition, before you leave Canada if possible.

If you do not meet either the green card or substantial presence tests, you may be able to meet to be treated as a resident alien taxpayer as long as you met the substantial presence test in following year (year X+1, where X = the tax year in question) and —

- you are present in the US for at least 31 days in a row in year X; and

- be present in the US for at least 75 percent of the time you were in the US in year X, beginning with the first day the 31-day period and ending 12/31/X.

If you make this election, you cannot file the tax return until you have met the substantial presence test for year X+1. For example, if you first came to the US on December 1, 2011, and remained in the US constantly thereafter, you would meet the substantial presence test on May 1, 2012, because February had 29 days in 2012, otherwise it would have been May 2. If you were out of the country at any time during the period, those days absent would increase the time required to meet the test. If you came to the US late in the year, you will have to file an extension and wait the necessary amount of time before filing the return. Under this election, the date of residency will generally begin your first day in the US. You will report only the income earned from that date to the end of the year on the tax return. The income before that period is reported on your Canadian return.

However, if the taxpayer is a dual-status taxpayer (remember, this is part year as a nonresident and part year as a resident), you can choose to be treated as a US resident for the entire year if *all* of the following apply:

- You were a nonresident alien at the beginning of the year.

- You were a resident at the end of the year.

- You are married to a US citizen or resident alien at the end of the year. If you are single at the end of the year, the election cannot be made.

- Your spouse also joins you in making the election.

When the election is made, both you and your spouse are treated as if you were resident of the US for the entire year, meaning you will have to report and pay tax on worldwide income for the entire year. There are two possible elections to be made:

- One that allows for you to file jointly.

- One that allows the resident spouse to treat the nonresident spouse as a resident.

You are probably thinking to yourself, why would I want to report all of my income to the US when I would normally have to report only the income I earned since moving to the US; wouldn't that cost me more in taxes? As we mention throughout the book, you will nearly always pay less tax as a US taxpayer than as a Canadian taxpayer. We go into the specifics as to why this is true in Chapter 9.

You might be saying, even if the US is less expensive, won't I be paying tax twice since I will be reporting the income earned in Canada, to Canada and to the US as well, if I make this election? The answer is that you will be reporting the income twice, but you will only be paying tax once because of the Treaty and foreign tax credits. While there can be unusual circumstances where it would not be better to make the election to be a US resident for the full year and report all of your income in the US, the large majority of the time the election will be to your benefit.

As a resident alien, you frequently continue to have income from Canada. Which country gets to tax that income and how it is taxed is spelled out in the Treaty. For example, the Treaty will prescribe the withholding rates for the different types of income. It will also spell out situations in which you or various types of income may be exempt from tax in one country or the other. (See Chapter 3, for a detailed discussion of the Treaty.)

Individuals generally cannot enter the US without being a US citizen, green card holder, or visa holder. The following are common immigration visas:

- Business Visitor Visa (B-1)
- Visitor for Pleasure (B-2)
- Treaty Trader (E-1)
- Treaty Investor (E-2)
- Student Visa (F-1)
- Dependent of Student (F-2)
- Professionals (H-1B)
- Seasonal Agricultural Work (H-2A)
- Unskilled Worker (H-2B)
- Nonimmigrant Trainees (H-3)
- Dependents of H Visa Holder (H-4)
- Exchange Visitor (J-1)
- Executive or Manager of Foreign Company (L-1)
- Listed in Treaty (TN)*

*Note: The North American Free Trade Agreement (NAFTA) came into effect January 1, 1994. NAFTA established an immigration category called Trade National (TN). It permits people to come in as nonimmigrants on the basis of being a "professional" listed on a schedule to NAFTA. The TN visa is valid for three years and may be renewed for an unlimited duration, as long as the visa holder maintains his or her nonimmigrant intent. The list of professionals include accountants, engineers, scientists, research assistants, medical and allied professionals, scientific technicians, disaster-relief insurance claims adjusters, architects, lawyers, economists computer systems analysts, management consultants, and others. Professionals require at least a Bachelor's degree.

Table 2 is a flowchart illustrating various immigration options and whether you are eligible for each option.

There are two business immigration categories: immigrant (permanent) and nonimmigrant (temporary). There are five preference levels within the employment-based immigration categories. The first preference is priority workers, second preference are professionals, third preference are skilled and unskilled workers, fourth preference are religious workers, and the fifth preference are immigrant investors.

If your intent is to obtain a green card and live the in the US permanently, at some point you will need to get onto the immigrant visa track so that you can progress from visa holder to green card holder and eventually citizenship, if you wish. For example, a TN visa and an H1-B visa are similar, but they are different in one important way, the TN visa does not lead to permanent residency, whereas the H1-B can.

Table 3 illustrates whether or not your status would be considered a nonresident alien or resident alien.

2. How Do I Get an Identification Number?

If you have entered the US on a work visa or Green Card, you are eligible for and should receive a Social Security Number (SSN). An SSN signals to employers that you are legally eligible to work in the US. The SSN is therefore restricted to only those people with certain types of visas or a Green Card. To apply for an SSN simply complete the Application for a Social Security Card (Form SS-5) and mail or take it to the nearest Social Security Administration office.

If you enter the US on a nonwork visa (typically as a spouse of someone who has entered on a work visa), you cannot receive an SSN and you will have to apply for what is called an Individual Taxpayer Identification Number (ITIN). The ITIN is generally not given out until there is a need to do so — typically for filing a tax return. In most cases, you will complete the Application for IRS Individual Taxpayer Identification Number (Form W-7) when you file your first tax return. Your tax return and the W-7 are filed simultaneously.

Table 2
US IMMIGRATION OPTIONS

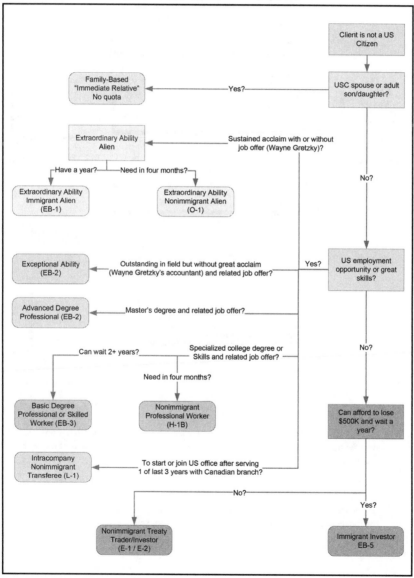

Table 3
YOUR STATUS: NONRESIDENT ALIEN OR RESIDENT ALIEN

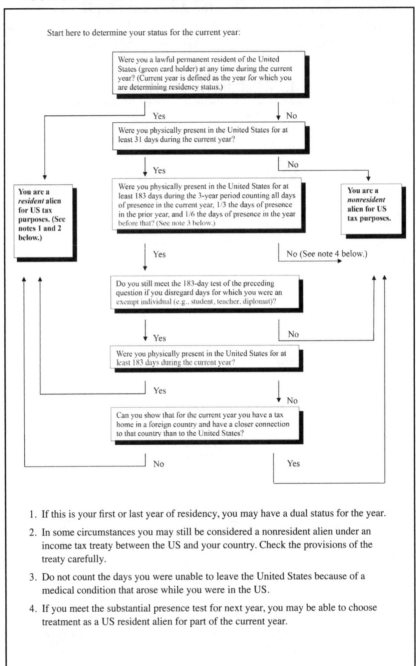

Start here to determine your status for the current year:

Were you a lawful permanent resident of the United States (green card holder) at any time during the current year? (Current year is defined as the year for which you are determining residency status.)

Yes / No

Were you physically present in the United States for at least 31 days during the current year?

Yes / No

You are a *resident* alien for US tax purposes. (See notes 1 and 2 below.)

Were you physically present in the United States for at least 183 days during the 3-year period counting all days of presence in the current year, 1/3 the days of presence in the prior year, and 1/6 the days of presence in the year before that? (See note 3 below.)

You are a *nonresident* alien for US tax purposes.

Yes / No (See note 4 below.)

Do you still meet the 183-day test of the preceding question if you disregard days for which you were an exempt individual (e.g., student, teacher, diplomat)?

Yes / No

Were you physically present in the United States for at least 183 days during the current year?

Yes / No

Can you show that for the current year you have a tax home in a foreign country and have a closer connection to that country than to the United States?

No / Yes

1. If this is your first or last year of residency, you may have a dual status for the year.

2. In some circumstances you may still be considered a nonresident alien under an income tax treaty between the US and your country. Check the provisions of the treaty carefully.

3. Do not count the days you were unable to leave the United States because of a medical condition that arose while you were in the US.

4. If you meet the substantial presence test for next year, you may be able to choose treatment as a US resident alien for part of the current year.

3

The Treaty

The Canada-US Treaty is formally known as the "Convention between Canada and the United States of America with Respect to Taxes on Income and on Capital" (hereafter referred to as the "Treaty") and exists primarily to prevent the same income being taxed by more than one country (double taxation). This can occur whenever you are a resident of one country and earn income in another country (e.g., you are living in the US and have interest, dividend, employment or business income, or pension income from Canada). These situations create a potential for double taxation because your country of residence, the US, and Canada have the right to tax the same income.

The Treaty also aids in the enforcement of the countries' tax laws by providing for exchanges of information between the different tax authorities and in some cases requires the other country to assist in the collection of tax due to the other country. For example, if you owe the IRS money and you move to Canada, in some cases Canada Revenue Agency (CRA) will be bound by the Treaty to assist in the collection efforts of the IRS, and vice versa.

Tax treaties include procedures for resolving differences of opinion between the countries on questions such as the taxation of a specific types of income, in which country the income was earned, or the tax residency of the taxpayer. In the Treaty, this is referred to as sending the issue to the "competent authority." Basically this means that the issue gets sent to the legal departments of the CRA and the IRS, they then decide who has the right to tax the individual or company. The result could be more significant than simply knowing who to write the check to because it could result in higher tax if one country gets to tax the income verses the other country.

Tax treaties are increasingly important in this era of increased globalization. Treaties provide dependable answers as to which country has the right to tax businesses that operate or invest abroad, new ventures that seek foreign investment and individuals who want to live or work in another country.

Canada was America's first treaty partner when, in 1936, The Reciprocal Tax Convention, came into force. The Reciprocal Tax Convention was in effect until 1941, and then it was replaced by the Canada-US Tax Convention. The current Treaty was signed on September 26, 1980. The Treaty has been amended by five protocols; the most recent became effective January 1, 2009.

Note: The time between when the Treaty is negotiated and signed, and when it is ratified by the respective governments can be significant. This difference in time can cause planning nightmares, as happened with the latest protocol when 15 months passed between the Treaty being signed and the governments ratifying them.

The Treaty is based on the model developed by the Organisation for Economic Co-operation and Development (OECD), but also includes some features that are unique to the Canada-US relationship. As cross-border situations evolve, the Treaty must also evolve to remain effective. The Treaty has been updated in 1983, 1984, 1995, 1997, and 2009. These changes to the Treaty, known as Protocols, ensure the Treaty has adopted the latest tax developments in each country, as well as the changing needs of Canadian and US individuals and businesses. The latest Protocol to the Treaty, the Fifth Protocol was signed on September 21, 2007, and came into force on January 1, 2009, after it was ratified by the Canadian and US governments.

The discussion in this chapter is not a technical interpretation of the Treaty, it is also not meant to be all encompassing, but rather to make readers aware of some Articles (Chapters) of the Treaty that relate to Canadians living in America.

The Treaty applies to residents of Canada and the US and applies to all taxes imposed under the *Income Tax Act* of Canada and to the income and estate taxes imposed by the US Internal Revenue Code. The Treaty also applies to the US accumulated earnings tax, personal holding company tax, US excise tax on private foundations, and social security taxes. Estate tax imposed by the US Internal Revenue Code was added to the third protocol to the Treaty and was previously not addressed.

Taxes imposed by the provinces in Canada and by the states of the US are not covered by the Treaty. In the US, each state has its own tax laws and some of the states will not directly accept the provisions of the Canada-US Tax Convention, but will indirectly accept them because their tax laws use as the starting point for tax computation, the federal adjusted gross income. Since the starting point is federal adjusted gross income, any income, deduction, or exclusion for US purposes will be allowed for state income tax purposes, unless otherwise specifically noted; one such state is Arizona. Some states do not accept the provisions of the Treaty because they have their own system of computing income; one such state is California. Some states, such as Michigan accept taxes paid to a Canadian province as a credit against the state tax.

Note: The point made above about some states indirectly allowing for the benefits of the Treaty and some not, is very important. One example that will be discussed in more detail in Chapter 6 is the taxation of RRSPs by Arizona and California. The Treaty allows the annual earnings of RRSPs to be deferred if the proper election and forms are filed. In a state like Arizona, if the deferral is properly made and thus is not part of the federal adjusted gross income, the income will not be included in Arizona and thus will also be deferred in Arizona. However, since the deferral has no effect in California, the annual earnings of your RRSP will be taxed if you live in California. The only ways around this issue are to not live in a state like California or to cash out your RRSPs.

So that you have an idea of what is addressed in the Treaty as well as to have a quick reference, Table 4 is the Table of Articles (Contents) of the Treaty. We will not discuss all of the Treaty Articles, but many of these topics have additional details in other chapters of this book (e.g., dividends and interest will be discussed in Chapter 7 on investments).

Table 4
TREATY ARTICLES

Article I:	Personal Scope
Article II:	Taxes Covered
Article III:	General Definitions
Article IV:	Residence
Article V:	Permanent Establishment
Article VI:	Income from Real Property
Article VII:	Business Profits
Article VIII:	Transportation
Article IX:	Related Persons
Article X:	Dividends
Article XI:	Interest
Article XII:	Royalties
Article XIII:	Gains
Article XIV:	Independent Personal Services
Article XV:	Dependent Personal Services
Article XVI:	Artistes and Athletes
Article XVII:	Withholding of Taxes in Respect to Independent Personal Services
Article XVIII:	Pensions and Annuities
Article XIX:	Government Service
Article XX:	Students
Article XXI:	Exempt Organizations
Article XXII:	Other Income

Note: The nondiscrimination provision basically prevents a country from taxing its noncitizens more than its citizens.

Beware that these general rules may be overridden by the "savings clause." The saving clause preserves the right of each country to tax its own residents as if no tax treaty were in effect. Thus, once you become a resident alien of the US, you generally lose any tax treaty benefits that relate to your US income. The saving clause may prohibit you from claiming certain Treaty benefits because you are a US citizen. One example is that capital gains are generally taxable, only in the country of residence. However, a US citizen living in Canada will still have to report all capital gains on his or her US tax return.

1. Residency

An individual or an entity such as a corporation or partnership is considered to be resident of a country if it is the individual's or entity's country of domicile, residence, place of management, place of incorporation, or other criteria of a similar nature. If you or an entity of yours is considered a resident, you and/or that entity will be subject to the taxes of that country; therefore, it is very important to know which country you are or your entity is a resident of.

US citizens are always taxed on their worldwide income, regardless of where they actually reside. US citizens that reside in Canada will also be taxed as Canadian residents, under the laws of Canada.

If you are a non-US citizen, you may spend time and have activities in both Canada and the US; in some of those circumstances, your tax residency may be in question. When an individual's residency status is question, the Treaty has tie-breaker rules in which to settle the issue.

The tie-breaker rules provide four questions for you to answer. If the answer to the first question does not clarify which country you are a resident of, go on to the next question, and so on until you can determine which country you are a resident of. Once you get a clear answer, stop, that is where you are a resident.

- Where is your permanent home?
- Where are your closest economic and personal relations?
- Where is your habitual abode (the country where you spend most of your time)?
- What country are you a citizen of?

If after answering these four questions you cannot determine where you are considered resident, then you can request that the "competent authorities" of Canada and the US settle the issue by Mutual Agreement. What this means is that the CRA and the IRS will get together and decide.

Businesses that operate on both sides of the border need to understand in which jurisdiction they will be taxed on their profits. The concept of "Permanent Establishment" is defined in the Treaty to determine which country has the right to tax the profits of the business. A permanent establishment for businesses is analogous to residency for individuals. For example, the profits of a business resident in Canada would be taxable in the US only to the extent that some or all of the profits are attributable to a permanent establishment in the US. A permanent establishment would include the following:

- Place of management

- Branch

- Office

- Factory

- Workshop

- Mine, oil or gas well, quarry, or other place of resource extraction

- Building or construction site that lasts more than 12 months

- Person acting on behalf of the resident of the other country if he or she has the authority to conclude contracts (not including independent agents)

A permanent establishment would not include a facility used solely for storage or warehousing, distribution, research, or advertising. It would also not include a business that uses a broker or an independent agent. A permanent establishment can also occur when a business in one country sends an employee to work in the other country for more than 183 days in any 12-month period, and more than 50 percent of the revenues of the business are derived from the services provided in the other country.

If there is a permanent establishment in the other country, the Treaty will tax the business profits as if the permanent establishment were a distinct and separate entity. That means that only the revenues generated and expenses incurred in that permanent establishment would determine the profits that would be subject to tax in the other country. In other words, if you have a Canadian business with a permanent establishment in the US, the profits of the US operations attributed to the permanent establishment in the US would be taxed in the US. Additionally the Treaty allows for the allocation of certain head office expenses, such as general administrative expenses, that would be allocable to the permanent establishment even though the expense was incurred in the other country.

The domestic tax rules of each country include the application of foreign tax credits (see Chapter 5 for more information), which is a mechanism to eliminate double tax. To take this example one step further, if you have a business in Canada that had a permanent establishment in the US, the US would tax the profits on the US operation only and Canada would tax the profits on the worldwide profits. The company would be allowed a foreign tax credit for the taxes paid to the US so that in the end, the tax paid in Canada, after credits, is only the tax on the Canadian profits.

2. Real Property

The Treaty directs that income derived from real property (real estate) situated in the other country may be taxed in the other country. Any rental income from the use of real property is taxed in the country where the property is located. Any sale of real property is also taxed in the country where the real property is located. As an example, when you moved to the US you did not sell your Canadian home and you decided to rent your home in Canada while you are living in the US. The profit on the rental income will be taxable in Canada. In addition, as a US resident, you must include the rental income in your world income. Any income tax you pay in Canada can be taken as a foreign tax credit on your US tax return. When you decide to sell your home, the same idea applies, you will be taxed in Canada and the US on the profit and a foreign tax credit is taken in the US to prevent double taxation.

The *Income Tax Act* (ITA) allows you an unlimited exemption for gain on your principal residence; however, any gain that occurs after the home is no longer your principal residence is taxable upon sale. The problem is that when it comes time to sell your home in the future, how do you determine that amount of gain since the time it was your principal residence? The answer is to get at least one (three would be better) "broker's opinion" as to the value of your home, as close as possible to your date of exit from Canada. The amount up to this value will be tax free as your principal residence; any price received above that amount will be taxable as a capital gain in Canada.

The taxation of a home that was, at some point, used as your principal residence in Canada, can be significantly different in the US and Canada. The main reason is that while Canada allows for an unlimited exemption of gain, the US allows for $250,000 per person ($500,000 per couple), if the home was your principal residence at least two out of the previous five years. So one way the taxation could be different is if the gain is greater than the $250,000 or $500,000, or the other way it could be different is if you have rented the Canadian home for four years or more after moving to the US. In this later case, you would lose the exemption all together.

The other way the tax could be different is when there is a change in the value of the currency. You could have a no gain or even a loss in the value of the home, but the currency could improve by the time you sell and you would have a gain that would have to be reported. This issue applies to everything, but is most pronounced in real estate because of the time span between purchase and sale.

For example, since we are trying to illustrate the effect of changes in the currency, let's assume there are no other factors to consider and let's say that you bought a cottage (not your principal residence) in Canada for C$200,000 in 2000. In 2011, you sold the cottage for the same C$200,000. Obviously, in Canada you would have no gain. However, assuming you were living in the US when you sold the cottage, your gain from a US perspective would be US$65,340. The reason for this is that when you bought the cottage in 2000, the annual average exchange rate was 1.48520240 Canadian dollars for each US dollar or .6733 US dollars for each Canadian dollar. This means that you bought the cottage for the equivalent of US$134,660. When you sold the cottage in 2011, the annual average exchange rate was .98906920 Canadian dollars for each US dollar or 1.011 US dollars for each Canadian dollar. This means that you sold the cottage for the equivalent of US$202,200, a gain of US$65,340.

3. Dividends, Interest, and Royalties

Dividends paid by a company in one country to a resident of the other country may be taxed in the other country. In addition, the country from which the payer of the dividend is resident can tax the dividend as well. What this means is that if you are living in the US and you receive a dividend from a Canadian company, there will be withholding in Canada (Canadian tax) and that dividend will have to be included in your US income and taxed accordingly (US tax). In every case where income is reported and subject to tax in both countries, a foreign tax credit is available to avoid double tax.

As we discuss in Chapter 4 the Canadian Taxation of Nonresidents, without the benefit of the Treaty, the withholding would be 25 percent, but because of the Treaty, the withholding is only 15 percent when paid to individuals. However, an intercorporate dividend paid between a parent corporation and its subsidiary that is resident in the other country will have only a 5 percent withholding tax.

Interest paid by a resident of one country to a resident of the other country after January 1, 2009, will only be taxed in the country of residence. The Fifth Protocol eliminated the nonresident withholding tax on interest, when the interest is paid as part of an arm's length transaction.

Most royalties are exempt from any withholding taxes, such as copyright royalties in respect of the production or reproduction of any literary, dramatic, musical, or artistic work. Royalties from motion pictures and works on film, videotape, or other means of reproduction for use in connection with television are subject to 10 percent withholding. Royalties for industrial equipment are subject to a 30 percent withholding.

4. Gains

The treaty provides different rules for capital gains from real property and for gains from other capital property. Generally, gains are taxable only in the country of residence, except that gains arising from real property are taxed in the country where the real property is located, and in the country of residence, as we have already discussed. Generally, all other gains, such as the gains you incur in your investment portfolio are not taxable in the country they occurred; they are taxable only in the country you are resident of.

The Treaty allows you to step up the basis in your assets when you move to the US because you are subject to a "deemed disposition" of your capital assets when leaving Canada. This deemed disposition assumes that you sell all of your assets except for your Canadian real estate and your retirement assets such as RRSPs. The gain that results in this deemed disposition is reported on your final Canadian tax return. If this provision did not exist in the Treaty, when you eventually sold those properties as resident of the US, you would have to pay tax again in the US, on the same assets. The Treaty states that if you are not subject to US tax at the time of emigration from Canada to the US, you can elect to adjust the cost basis in those assets to fair market value at the date of the deemed disposition. Therefore, this "step up" in basis for US tax purposes ensures that only the post-emigration gain will be subject to US tax.

Warning: The ability to step up your cost basis is granted by the Treaty. You must make an election on your first US tax return, using Form 8833 (Treaty Election). The step up is not automatic; failure to make the election will cause double tax. You may *not* want to make the election to step up your basis if you have a net loss on your assets when you exited Canada. You cannot pick and choose which assets to step up, it is a decision that is made across the board for all assets that are subject to the deemed disposition tax.

US citizens that were residents of Canada that immigrate to the US also have a problem since the deemed disposition of their assets upon emigrating from Canada is not a US tax issue so you end up with a timing mismatch. The Treaty alleviates this problem as well by allowing a step in basis on the property to the value equal to the fair market value at the date of emigration. The US citizens are allowed to report the difference between their cost and fair market value at emigration and report the gain, which would then be allowed the foreign tax paid to Canada to offset the US tax on the gain.

Further, the US citizen is deemed to have repurchased the property at an amount equal to its fair market value at the time so, in essence, only the post-emigration gain will be taxed in the US. The problem with this option is where does the cash to pay the tax come from? Most times the best solution is to actually sell the assets, since you have to pay Canadian tax anyway. By selling the assets this will trigger a US tax on the gain, but you now have the cash to pay the tax and if you really like the asset, you can always buy it back.

5. Personal Services

If you are living in the US and receive employment income (or self-employment income) for services performed in Canada, the income is exempt from tax in Canada if the income does not exceed $10,000 in the source country currency. Alternatively, the income is also exempt in the source country (Canada, in this case) if you were not present in Canada for more than 183 days in any 12-month period and that the income is not "borne by" a person or business (or permanent establishment) that is resident in the source country. The term "borne by" means allowable as a deduction in computing taxable income. The simple reason for this is that if someone or some business is deducting the employment expense, someone has to report the offsetting amount of income. Likewise, if the expense is not being claimed in Canada, there is no need to report the income.

6. Artists and Athletes

Income of an artist or athlete may be taxed in the source country where the gross revenue exceeds $15,000 in the currency of the source country. For example, if a musician that is a resident of the US performs in a concert in Canada and receives more than C$15,000 (gross, before expenses), the musician must report and pay tax in Canada on all of the income (less expenses). The musician does not simply report the amount above the C$15,000 threshold; $15,000 or less is exempt, $15,001 and greater is taxable. The gross receipts would include all expense reimbursements. The US resident musician would also include her US receipts and expenses in her Canadian tax return and she would receive a credit against her Canadian tax for taxes paid in the US.

An entertainer would include a theater, motion picture, radio, or television artist. In order to qualify as an artist or entertainer, the taxpayer must generally "provide the performance that the audience seeks to experience." There was a case in Canada of a play-by-play personality who claimed that he was an entertainer and the court ruled that he was not an artist for purposes of this article of the Treaty, but rather a radio journalist.

The Treaty also treats the income of artists and athletes as being earned by the artist and athlete regardless of whether the income is earned directly or indirectly through some type of entity, such as a corporation. Therefore, in the example above, if the US resident musician earned the income from a concert in Canada through a corporation, the corporation would pay tax in Canada on the income earned in Canada.

These rules do not apply to an athlete who is employed by a team that participates in a league, such as the National Hockey League or Major League Baseball. Therefore, a US resident hockey player who earns a salary from a US hockey team would be exempt from Canadian taxation if he was not present in Canada for more than 183 days in any 12-month period and his remuneration was not borne by a team in Canada and the team did not have a permanent establishment in Canada (or the income earned was less than C$10,000).

Chapter 4 provides additional information regarding actors providing film or video services.

7. Pensions and Annuities

An important article of the Treaty that seniors should be interested in is the article that pertains to pensions and annuities. The tax treatment of pensions and annuities in one country is respected by the other country. This means that if you receive a pension or an annuity in the US that is partially taxable and partially tax free, Canada will treat it the same way. Company or government pensions and annuities are subject to a 15 percent nonresident withholding tax. The term pension, as it is used in the Treaty means a company or government retirement benefit for employment services performed. The Treaty defines an annuity as "a stated sum paid periodically at stated times during the life or during a specified number of years, under an obligation to make payments."

Though the Treaty treats IRAs (including Roth IRAs) and RRSPs as pensions, Registered Savings plans are taxed differently than company and government pensions and annuities. Withdrawals from an RRSP are always considered a lump-sum distribution and subject to 25 percent withholding. Withdrawals from an RRIF can be either a lump-sum or periodic. Lump-sum distributions are subject to 25 percent withholding and periodic payments are subject to 15 percent withholding. (A periodic distribution has a specific definition, see Chapter 6 for the definition.) The last thing we will note here is that Registered Savings plans have special reporting requirements in the US, whereas a pension generally does not.

US retirement accounts can generally be broken down into employer-sponsored plans such as 401(k), 403(b), profit-sharing plans, defined benefit retirement plans, and Individual Retirement Accounts (IRAs), such as a traditional IRA and Roth IRA. There are other types of accounts, but these are the most common. A traditional IRA is analogous to an RRSP; you contribute money to an account you control, up to a certain limit. Contributions up to the limit are tax deductible and continue to be deferred until withdrawn. Minimum distributions are required beginning in the year you turn age 70.5.

The big difference between an RRSP and IRA is the contribution limits. For 2012, the contribution limit for an RRSP is C$22,970, while the contribution limit for an IRA is $5,000 if you are younger than 50 and \$6,000 if you are 50 or older. Another big difference is that while you can carry over any unused RRSP contributions you did not make, in the US there is a "use it or lose it rule"— you are not able to carry over your unused contributions.

A Roth IRA is similar to a Tax-Free Savings Account (TFSA), where you receive no deduction for contributions, but the money comes out tax free. A TFSA creates a number of additional reporting issues in the US. It may not be worth keeping the TFSA because of the additional tax preparation costs. Additionally, because the income earned in the TFSA is not tax free in the US, we recommend liquidating the TFSA before coming to the US, or if you are already in the US, as soon as possible.

The Fifth Protocol tried to create parity in the treatment of retirement plans between the US and Canada. A qualified contribution and deduction in one country qualifies as a deduction in the other country, subject to the limits of that country. For example, if a Canadian resident, US citizen contributes more than \$5,000 or \$6,000 to his or her RRSP, only the \$5,000 or \$6,000, if older than 50, will be deductible. Per the Treaty, the plans also retain the tax characteristics in the other country. For example, a Roth IRA continues to be tax deferred and withdrawals continue to be tax free for Canadian residents. One exception to this is the TFSA; it is not identified in the Treaty as a "pension" and it is therefore not covered by the Treaty and by default is taxable in the US.

8. Social Security

Social Security benefits paid by Canada in the form of Canada or Quebec pension (CPP or QPP) and Old Age Security (OAS) and Social Security benefits paid by the US are taxable only in the country of residence. Because the benefits are taxable only in the country of residence, there is no withholding by the country paying the benefits. In the US, your Canadian benefits are taxed the same as US social security is taxed in the US. For Americans living in Canada receiving US social security, the benefits are only 85 percent taxable in Canada.

Canadians who attain the age of 65 years of age are entitled to receive OAS which is based on the number of years after age 18 that the applicants have resided in Canada. In order to receive the full entitlement, the applicants have to have resided in Canada for

20 years after age 18. If the applicants have resided in Canada after age 18 for at least ten years, they can receive an OAS pension if they reside outside Canada.

The US-Canada Agreement on Social Security allows you to count the years you contributed to the US Social Security system, to count as years of residency in Canada for purposes of qualifying for OAS.

As a resident of Canada receiving OAS, you will have $0.15 of every dollar of your benefit clawed back, if your income is greater than $69,562 (in 2012). As a resident of the US, you are not subject to the clawback and receive the maximum monthly benefit of C$540.12 (2012), if you qualify under the rules above.

9. Government Service

Employees of foreign governments are taxable in their home country. As an example, an employee of a Canadian consulate office in the US would only be taxable as a resident of Canada and would not be taxable in the US provided the employee was also not a US citizen. If the employee was a US citizen, he or she would be taxed in Canada on his or her earnings in Canada as a nonresident of Canada and would also be taxed in the US on that income and would receive a credit against US taxes for the tax paid to Canada.

10. Students

Under the Treaty an individual who normally resides in one country and becomes a full-time student, apprentice, or business trainee in the other country would be exempt from tax on payments received from his or her country of residence. A Canadian resident who attends school in the US would be exempt from tax on any amounts received for the student's maintenance, education, or training from Canada. Any income earned by the student in the US through employment would naturally be taxable in the US.

11. Taxes Imposed by Reason of Death

The Treaty includes rules to coordinate the death tax regimes of each country. The US imposes an estate tax at death, which is a tax on the fair market value of assets owned by the decedent (the person who died) at death. Canada imposes an income tax on the accrued gain of assets to the date of death. (We have devoted an entire chapter to US Estate and Gift Tax; please read Chapter 10 for more details.)

One thing that confuses many people including professionals is the estate tax exemption allowed to US residents. Residents of the US have the same exemption as US citizens. In 2012, that amount is $5,120,000. The US citizen gets an unlimited marital deduction, but a noncitizen resident does not. This means that if your estate exceeds the exemption, a US citizen can receive an unlimited amount for a deceased spouse, whereas a non-US citizen can only receive the exemption amount tax free. Nonresidents are generally allowed a $60,000 exemption. The Treaty allows for a pro-rata exemption based on your US assets to your worldwide assets. Note: Your worldwide assets include the death benefit of your life insurance.

The other important feature of this section of the Treaty is to provide a tax credit for death taxes paid to the other country. While there are some important exceptions to this credit (see Chapter 10), generally speaking, if you have assets in both countries and death taxes are paid in both countries, there will be a credit allowed for the other country's tax.

Table 5 includes a summary of the various types of income and the withholding rates.

Table 5
TYPES OF INCOME AND WITHOLDING RATES

Types of Income	Withholding Rates
Wages	Withholding is done through the paycheck in the typical way
Interest	0 percent if an arm's length transaction
Dividends	15 percent (5 percent for payments of subsidiary to parent corporation)
Royalties	0 percent (TV or film 10 percent and Industrial Equipment 30 percent)
Rents	30 percent on gross rents
Gains (non-real property)	Gains (non-real property); generally taxable only in the country of residence
Pensions and Annuities	15 percent
Social Security	0 percent

4

Canadian Taxation of Nonresidents

Now that you are living in the US and have exited Canada, you are subject to Canada's nonresident tax rules, which is Part XIII of the *Income Tax Act* (ITA). The *Income Tax Act* of Canada is divided into 17 parts that consist of tax laws related to the reporting of income, the calculation of taxes as well as collection and enforcement procedures. We will only be concerned with two of those parts, Part I having to do with income tax, and Part XIII having to do with the taxation of income of Canadian nonresidents.

As Canadians, you are most familiar with Part I of the *Income Tax Act*, which is the authority for requiring the filing of income tax returns, the computation, the calculation of income tax, and its enforcement. Since this book is not on the taxation of Canadians in Canada, but is instead a book on the taxation of Canadians in the US, we will not be discussing Part I of the act but will instead focus on Part XIII of the *Income Tax Act* of Canada, titled, "Taxation of Income from Canada of Nonresident Persons." Canadians living in the US will almost always be nonresidents of Canada and therefore subject to Part XIII for income earned in Canada.

Part XIII imposes a withholding tax on income paid to nonresidents of Canada. These amounts include pensions, annuities, management fees, interest, dividends, rents, royalties, estate or trust income, and film or acting services. The default withholding percentage is 25 percent unless the amount is reduced by the Treaty. The current Treaty came into force in 1984 and there have been numerous changes since that time which are referred to as Protocols (amendments). The Treaty provides withholding rates for all types of income. The withholding rates range from 0 percent (not taxable) to 25 percent (no reduction in the default withholding rate).

The Canada Revenue Agency (CRA) provides an online calculator for determining the correct withholding. The problem we found with it is that it assumes you know the meaning of the terms used. For example, the drop down menu asks if the income item is a lump-sum or a periodic payment. These items have specific definitions and if you choose the wrong item, you will get the wrong answer. Here is the site www.cra.gc.ca/partxiii-calculator.

1. Who Is Considered a Nonresident of Canada?

Section 250 of the *Income Tax Act* (ITA) provides the definitions of resident and nonresident. You are a nonresident of Canada if you reside in another country (the US) or do not have residential ties to Canada and you live outside of Canada throughout the year or you stay in Canada for less than 183 days in a year. The exception to this would be if you live outside of Canada because you are an employee of the government of Canada. For example, an employee of the Ministry of Foreign Affairs who works at a Canadian consulate outside of Canada would be classified as a resident of Canada along with his or her spouse and family members that reside with him or her outside of Canada. Other examples would be members of the Canadian Forces or those working under a Canadian International Development Agency (CIDA) program. These types of individuals would be classified as "deemed residents" of Canada. A deemed resident of Canada also includes those who spend more than 183 days in Canada in a year and are not considered a resident of another country under a tax treaty. All these individuals would be taxed in Canada on their world income.

Note: The Treaty forces you to be a resident of one country or the other; you cannot be a resident of both countries or a nonresident of both countries, assuming you are not a resident of another country.

Residential ties refer to numerous factors that have been developed through case law over the years. These primary factors include the following:

- Home in Canada

- Spouse and dependents in Canada

- Personal property such as a vehicle or furniture in Canada

- Social ties in Canada would include items such as membership in golf clubs or membership in religious organizations

Other secondary factors would include:

- A driver's license issued by a province or territory in Canada

- Bank accounts and/or investments accounts in Canada as well as Canadian credit cards

- Health insurance with a Canadian province or Territory

The Treaty includes provisions that determine in which country you are a resident. These include tie-breaker rules to help determine your residency. (This is discussed in more detail in Chapter 3.)

This chapter deals with persons that are specifically nonresidents of Canada and earning income from Canada. As a nonresident of Canada you will pay tax on income received from sources in Canada. The type of tax you will have to pay and the requirement to file a Canadian income tax return will depend on the type of income received.

Nonresidents of Canada are subject to tax under Part I or Part XIII of the Income Tax Act. You will be subject to Part I tax and will have to file a Canadian tax return if you receive the following types of income:

- Income from employment in Canada or carrying on a business in Canada

- Receipt of Canadian scholarships, fellowships, bursaries, and research grants

- Income from providing services in Canada other than in the course of employment

- Disposing of certain Canadian property

If you receive income from Canada that is subject to Part XIII tax, you do not need to file a Canadian income tax return. However, in some limited situations, it may be advantageous to file a Canadian return and pay tax under Part I of the ITA. There are three situations in which the nonresident can elect to file a tax return (which is discussed later in this section).

Part XIII tax is withheld (deducted) by the payer; you receive the net amount, after tax. Canadian payers, including financial institutions, must deduct Part XIII tax and remit it to the CRA. In most cases, the Part XIII tax is the final tax liability to Canada on this income and no additional reporting is required in Canada, assuming the correct amount of tax was withheld.

It is your responsibility to notify your financial institutions and the government that you are a nonresident of Canada so that they can withhold the correct amount of tax. If you fail to notify them and no tax is withheld (or not enough tax is withheld), you are responsible for the extra tax, but more importantly, you will be subject to penalties and interest for underpayment of tax. We recommend sending a letter or email stating that you are a nonresident rather than simply calling. If there is a dispute, you will have proof that you told the institution and it now becomes the institution's responsibility if the tax is not withheld.

The most common types of Canadian source income that is subject to Part XIII tax include:

- Dividends
- Rental and royalty payments
- Pension payments
- Retiring allowances
- Registered Retirement Savings Plan payments
- Registered Retirement Income Fund payments
- Annuity payments
- Management fees

It should be noted that interest income received or credited to a nonresident is exempt from Canadian Part XIII tax as long as the payer is unrelated to the nonresident; this is referred to as an arm's length transaction. Canada Pension Plan (CPP), Quebec Pension Plan (QPP), and Old Age Security (OAS) are also exempt from withholding per the Treaty.

Part XIII tax is not refundable. You do not file an income tax return unless you are in one of the three situations you can elect to file a return. You can obtain a refund of Part XIII tax, only if an incorrect amount was withheld. An example of a situation where this happens is when a financial institution withholds 30 percent on a RRIF payment instead of 15 percent. If a situation like this happens, you will need to file Form NR7-R (Application for Refund of Part XIII Tax Withheld) to obtain a refund. Filing the NR7-R is a long procedure and it can take CRA in excess of a year to process the NR7-R and issue the refund. It is wise to be in contact with the payer ahead of time to ensure that the payer is indeed withholding the correct amount of Part XIII tax.

The first of the three exceptions to filing a Canadian tax return under Part XIII relates to the receipt of rental income earned from a property situated in Canada. Under Part XIII the tenant or manager of the property should remit 25 percent of the gross rental received or credited to the nonresident. This tax is due by the 15th of the month following the date the rent was received or credited to the nonresident. Any late payments of the Part XIII tax will incur interest charges. Under the usual rules of Part XIII the payment of this tax would end your tax obligation to Canada. An annual reporting form NR4 (Statement of Amounts Paid or Credited to Nonresidents of Canada) would be issued to the nonresident indicating the gross rents earned and the Part XIII tax that was remitted to the CRA on behalf of the nonresident.

However, you can elect to file under Section 216 of the *Income Tax Act* to pay tax on the net rental income (after deducting rental expenses) rather than the gross rents. When you elect under section 216, you are electing to file a "special" return that is known as a "216 return." The return is due by June 30 of the following year. A late-filed 216 return may invalidate the election and thus you would owe Part XIII tax of 25 percent of the gross rental income instead of paying Part I tax on the net rental income.

In order to have Part XIII tax withheld on your net rental income, you must have an agent who could be any Canadian resident who acts on your behalf regarding the rental property. The NR6 (Undertaking to File an Income Tax Return by a Nonresident Receiving Rent from Real Property or Receiving a Timber Royalty) is due on or before January of each year or before the first rental payment is due. The NR6 would include an estimate of the upcoming year's gross rental income and an estimate of the upcoming year's rental expenses. The NR6 must be signed by the nonresident as well as by his or her agent prior to sending it to the CRA. After it's approved, you must file the Income Tax Return for Electing Under Section 216 (Form T1159) return to report your rental income and pay any tax due; the return must be filed by June 30 of the following year.

The second exception is for actors. If you are an actor living in the US and working in Canada, Part XIII says any nonresident individual or a foreign corporation related to that individual that provides acting services in Canada for a film or video shall have 23 percent of any amount paid withheld and that amount will be the final tax liability to Canada for those acting services. The withholding applies to fees for acting services, per diem payments for days in Canada, and similar benefits. This withholding is not required for reasonable travel expenses paid directly to third parties such as hotels and airlines and reasonable travel expenses reimbursed to the actor as long as they are supported by receipts.

As an actor, you can elect to file a return on a net Canadian source acting income at graduated individual or corporate rates instead of paying 23 percent tax on the gross income. In other words, you will be allowed to deduct acting expenses from your gross acting income and pay tax on the net income earned from your acting while in Canada. The amount withheld will be credited so that you or the corporation can receive a refund of any excess tax withheld.

The return is called a 216.1 return and is due by April 30 for individuals, or if you are self-employed, by June 15. However, if there is any tax due, it is due by April 30 even though the return does not have to be filed until later. If the entity is a corporation, the return is six months from the fiscal year end. If this return is filed late, then the election is invalid and the tax of 23 percent on the gross income from acting would be due.

We recommend that if you intend to file this return and make the election so as to pay tax on the net income from acting, that you apply to the CRA prior to providing the acting service in Canada, so that you can have the withholding rate reduced.

The third exception to filing a return is by filing a 217 election. There are only certain types of income eligible for a section 217 election and they are as follows:

- Old Age Security

- Canada Pension Plan

- Quebec Pension Plan

- Most superannuation and pension benefits

- Most registered retirement savings plan payments

- Most registered retirement income fund payments

- Death benefits

- Certain retiring allowances

- Registered supplementary unemployment benefit plan payments

- Most deferred profit-sharing plan payments

- Amounts received from a retirement compensation arrangement

- Prescribed benefits under a government assistance program

- Auto Pact benefits

Note: Because the withholding on these payments are typically 15 percent, you must report it on Schedule A (Statement of World Income). While your world income is not taxed, the world income is used to determine the allowable federal nonrefundable tax credits. If your world income is too high, you will have no tax credits and you will pay more under a 217 return than the withholding tax.

If you intend to file a 217 return on income, but it is not yet time to file it, you can apply to have CRA reduce the Part XIII tax. You will need to file an Application by a Nonresident of Canada for a Reduction in the Amount of Nonresident Tax Required to be Withheld (Form NR5) on or before October 1 or before the first payment to the nonresident is due. If the NR5 is approved by the CRA then the individual must file a section 217 return for each year of the approval period.

The CRA will use the information given on the form NR5 to determine if the election will be beneficial. If it is, the CRA will authorize the Canadian payer to reduce the amount of Part XIII nonresident withholding tax.

2. Selling Property in Canada

Although not subject to Part XIII tax, the balance of this chapter will deal with nonresidents of Canada selling property in Canada or more specifically, taxable Canadian property. Taxable Canadian property includes the following:

- Canadian real or immovable property

- Life insurance policies in Canada

- Canadian resource property

- Canadian timber resource property

- Depreciable property that is taxable Canadian property

- Business property used in Canada, shares of a private corporation where more than 50 percent of the fair market value was derived from any of the above mentioned during the previous five years, and shares of a public corporation where at any time in the previous five years the taxpayer holds more than 25 percent of the issued shares and derived more than 50 percent of its fair market value from any of the above mentioned.

The sale of other types of property, most commonly securities, is only taxable in the country of residence, per the Treaty. The exception to this is that US citizens are taxable on their world income and will therefore have to report the sale of securities on their US tax returns, even if they are living in Canada.

The CRA should be notified of the sale of taxable Canadian property in advance of the sale, but they must be notified no later than ten days after the closing of the sale. This usually happens when you receive a signed agreement on the sale of your property and a request is made to the CRA for a Certificate of Compliance Related to the Disposition of Taxable Canadian Property. When making this request, you report the selling price of the property, and the adjusted cost base of the property. The adjusted cost base would be the amount paid for the property and all subsequent improvements made to the property. All of the details regarding the sale price and adjusted cost base should be sent with the request. After CRA has reviewed the request, it will then request payment of 25 percent of the estimated gain, rather than 25 percent of the gross sales price.

If the Certificate of Compliance has not been received by the time the sale is completed, the lawyer for the vendor must withhold 25 percent of the purchase price in a trust account until the Compliance Certificate is received.

You must still file a Canadian tax return under Part I of the *Income Tax Act* of Canada for the year in which the sale took place. When you file, include any costs of disposition such as legal fees, real estate commissions, accounting fees, etc. This would normally result in a tax refund since these items are not included in the filing for the Compliance Certificate.

It should be noted that if the property was the taxpayer's principal residence, these procedures are still required. A principal residence is a housing unit normally inhabited by the taxpayer. A taxpayer who emigrates from Canada can designate a principal residence until he or she is no longer a resident of Canada. The effect of this is that there will be no capital gains tax on any accrued gains of a principal residence until the taxpayer emigrates from Canada; any gains accrued after his or her exit from Canada will be taxable.

If you are selling your former principal residence, you will designate that property as such in the request for the Compliance Certificate, so that a portion of the gain will be tax exempt. The problem is how will the CRA know the appreciation occurred after you emigrated from Canada? The answer is that the CRA won't unless you have documentation as to what the property was worth on or around the time you emigrated. The easiest way to document the value is to have one, or preferably three real estate agents provide you with a broker's opinion as the value of the home. We recommend that you do this as close to the date emigration as possible.

Note: Complications can arise when you have a typically large lot, including farms, or where you rented your home after you emigrated. Consult with a tax specialist before you sell the property so that you can estimate the tax consequences before the sale.

5

Foreign Tax Credits

Your income is at risk, two or more countries may want to tax you on the same income. You could be subject to tax in two countries in a number of scenarios, but they all boil down to one basic idea. When you live in a country that imposes taxes on worldwide income, such as the US or Canada, and you pay taxes in another (foreign) country because of income you earned in that foreign country, you can potentially be subject to double tax. If everyone wants a piece of your hard-earned money, how do you avoid paying taxes more than once? The good news is that you have two options. The first option is discussed in Chapter 3 (The Treaty), which provides specifics about which country gets to tax what income. The primary goal of the Treaty is to prevent double taxation. The second option to avoid double taxation is through foreign tax credits, which is the topic of this chapter.

Note: Some retail tax software packages do not handle foreign tax credits properly. Of course, since you are not an expert on foreign tax credits, you have no way of knowing whether your software handles them correctly or not. To make matters worse, there are other cross-border issues a retail software package may not address or may handle improperly.

As we mentioned in the introduction, we have been preparing complex tax returns for more 20 years and we are still amazed at the number of people who tell us that they have a simple situation. We want to let you in on a secret, if you are reading this book, you do not have a simple situation. We recommend that you seek a professional that is experienced with cross-border taxes. The professional will have the experience, know-how, and resources (professional software) to do the job properly.

1. What Are Foreign Tax Credits?

The definition of a tax credit is an item that reduces your actual tax. It differs from a tax deduction that reduces only your taxable income. A foreign tax credit is defined as a subtraction against federal income tax for a taxpayer who has paid taxes to another country on income that was also taxed in his or her home country. The foreign tax credit is calculated on IRS Form 1116 (Foreign Tax Credit) and flows through to page two (line 47 of the 2011 Form 1040 — US Individual Tax Return) of your personal tax return. Though we will not discuss the topic in this book, the foreign tax credit form for a corporation is Form 1118 (Foreign Tax Credits - Corporations).

There are two types of tax credits in the US, refundable and non-refundable. A refundable credit is defined as a tax credit that is not limited by tha amount of an individual's tax liability, meaning that you could receive a refund even when no tax has been paid. A refundable credit can turn your tax negative, meaning that you could receive a refund even when no tax is owed. However, most credits are nonrefundable, which means that the credit can only reduce the tax liability to zero. Foreign tax credits are nonrefundable.

The first thing to know about foreign tax credits is that you have to have income that is actually taxed (paid or accrued) in two or more countries. Unfortunately, not all types of taxes qualify for a foreign tax credit. To be a creditable tax, the tax has to be —

- imposed on you or, if filing jointly, your spouse, and not on someone else such as your children;

- paid or if it is not paid, it must be a legitimate liability that you will pay for that tax year (accrued); for example, if you had foreign income which had no withholding during the year (2012). The tax that you pay when you file your foreign tax return in 2013 still counts as a credit in 2012;

- an income tax or a tax similar to an income tax; and/or

- not imposed by a sanctioned country such as Iran, North Korea, or Syria.

Some taxes are not income taxes and will therefore not qualify for a tax credit. These include social security tax, sales tax, value added tax (VAT), and customs tax. An example of a tax that is similar to an income tax is a withholding tax.

You have two choices when foreign taxes are paid (or accrued). You can take the tax paid as a credit or as a deduction. The deduction is taken on Schedule A as an itemized deduction. (Chapter 8, Common Deductions, explains in more detail what an itemized deduction is and which expenses can be deducted.) A deduction reduces your income that is subject to tax and is not a direct subtraction on your tax. The benefit of a deduction is based on the highest tax bracket to which you are subject to; this is known as your marginal tax rate. For example, if you are in the 25 percent marginal tax bracket, you will reduce your tax $1 for every $4 of tax deducted. However, a credit is a dollar-for-dollar offset of your tax, so for every $1 of credit, you will reduce your tax by $1. The catch is that you may not get to use every dollar of foreign tax paid as a credit because of various limitations that we will explain shortly.

If a deduction only provides a partial benefit for the foreign tax you pay and a credit is a dollar-for-dollar reduction in tax, why would anyone ever take the tax as a deduction? We hope the following examples will help to explain why in some circumstances, taking the deduction may be the best choice.

Credit Example

Let's say you have $10,000 of foreign (Canadian) income, which results in $1,500 (15 percent) of US tax before credits. You also have $1,000 of taxes paid to Canada (foreign tax). The $1,000 paid to Canada becomes a foreign tax credit. If you choose the credit for the foreign tax paid (assuming you were able to use all $1,000 of the credit), your net US tax would be $500 ($1,500 minus the credit of $1,000). Note that you may not be able to use all of the $1,000 foreign tax paid in the year paid.

Deduction Example

Now take the same scenario and run it through the deduction model. Your income would be reduced to $9,000, from $10,000 because of the $1,000 of foreign tax you paid. Your tax would now be $1,350 ($9,000 x 15 percent). In other words, the benefit you receive from taking the deduction is only $150. Thought of a different way, you take the foreign tax of $1,000, times the 15 percent tax rate to get $150.

If the net tax is $500 for a credit and $1,350 for a deduction, why would anyone choose to take the deduction? In nearly every case you would chose the credit, but there are times why it is better to take the deduction. For instance, you might choose to take the deduction instead of the credit if you are unable to use all of your foreign tax paid, as a credit, in its entirety. This happens when the two countries tax income differently or at substantially different rates.

An example would be if you sold assets in Canada that were taxed differently in the US, resulting in a much larger gain in Canada than in the US. This can happen in a number of ways, such as different depreciation (capital cost allowance) amounts taken, or a portion of the gain is excluded in one country or another, or due to a change in currency.

For example, you withdrew $100,000 from your Registered Retirement Savings Plan (RRSP) and paid $25,000 in Canadian withholding tax. Furthermore, the US cost basis is $90,000 and your US tax is $1,500 on the $10,000 that is taxable in the US. Since the tax credit cannot exceed the US tax (remember it is a nonrefundable tax), the maximum credit is $1,500. In this case, you will have to carry $23,500 of credits forward for up to ten years; this is called a "credit carry forward." You may or may not be able to use this credit in future years. However, if you took the deduction of $25,000, you would have reduced your taxes by $3,750 ($25,000 x 15 percent), a benefit that exceeds the credit by $2,250.

Even in this case, it is not clear what the best option is. You might be able to use some or all of the $23,500 foreign tax credit carry forward during the next ten years. To do this you would have to generate significant foreign income over those years because you can only use the foreign tax credit to the extent that you have foreign income.

As a rule, you would typically choose the deduction over the credit when the scenario is similar to the one above and where you would be using the money from the RRSP (e.g., to buy a house) and therefore the money would not be available to produce foreign income going forward.

Note: If you think that Form 1116 (Foreign Tax Credit) looks dizzyingly complex, don't feel bad, it is. If you are completing this form yourself, please read the instructions and Publication 514 very carefully.

2. Types of Foreign Income

As you will see at the top of IRS Foreign Tax Credit (Form 1116), there are five different foreign income categories, but only two of them are used on a regular basis — passive category income and general category income. The segregation is to prevent a taxpayer from manipulating investments and averaging foreign tax credits on operating income, which generally have relatively high foreign tax rates imposed, with foreign tax credits on passive types of income. These latter types of income can often be invested in a way that allows for a low foreign tax. By segregating passive foreign source income and active foreign income into separate baskets in applying the foreign tax credit limitation, the tax law prevents cross-crediting of foreign taxes between operating and investment income.

"General limitation income" is anything that does not fall into one of the other categories. The most common types of general limitation income are wages, self-employment income, company pensions, and even income that would normally be passive.

"Passive income" includes dividends, interest, rents, royalties, annuities, and capital gains. There is, however, an exception called the "high tax kick out." This exception occurs when the foreign tax is higher than the highest US tax that can be imposed on that income. When this happens, income that would normally be passive will be moved to the general limitation category. To be clear, it is not the US tax that is actually imposed, but instead, it is the tax that theoretically can be imposed. For example, if the foreign tax paid on the foreign income is equal to or greater than 35 percent (in 2012, this is the highest US marginal tax rate), it will be subject to the high tax kick out.

Note: Foreign tax credits are subject to limitations per category. Each category is limited to the foreign income in that category, divided by worldwide income.

$$\text{FTC} = \text{Foreign Tax on Passive Income} \times \frac{\text{Foreign Passive Income}}{\text{World Income}}$$

If you are taking the foreign taxes paid as a credit on the federal return, you must do the same on the state return as well. Keep in mind that most states do not allow a credit for taxes paid to another country.

3. How to Calculate the Foreign Tax Credit

When taking the credit, you are asked to choose between "paid" or "accrued." We recommend that you choose accrued. Why? If you choose "paid," you are choosing the "cash method" of accounting. The cash method of accounting records income when cash is received and expenses when cash is paid out. This means that if you had withholding throughout the year, only those taxes could be taken as a credit for that year, and additional taxes due with the return (the following year) would have to be claimed on next year's return. If you received a refund, you would have to amend the previous year's return to reduce the credit taken for that year — too complicated, in our opinion, and therefore should be avoided.

Intuitively, you would think if you paid $100 in foreign tax that you would get $100 in foreign tax credits, but that is not always the case. The reason for this is that you can only take a credit against your foreign income. The maximum foreign tax credit is equal to the total US tax, times total foreign income, divided by your total world income. This ratio is applied separately to each type of foreign income then added together for a total. This can have the effect of reducing the total possible tax credit. Though the actual calculation of the foreign tax credit is more complicated in a number of ways, the following example below is used to illustrate the concept; the actual tax credit might ultimately be less than the example.

- Assume that you have $25,000 of wages (general limitation income) and $10,000 of dividends (passive income) from Canada and you have another $65,000 of US income (type does not matter), for a total income of $100,000. Further, you paid $10,000 of Canadian tax on the wages and $1,500 of

Canadian withholding on the dividends, for a total tax paid to Canada of $11,500. Your US tax before credits is $25,000. If you were able to aggregate income and foreign taxes the calculation would be $25,000 X $35,000/$100,000 = $8,750 (FTC) and $2,750 would be carried over.

When you split the amount out into separate buckets as required, you get the following:

- General limitation: $25,000 X $25,000/$100,000 = $6,250 with $3,750 carried over in the general limitation category.

- Passive income: $25,000 X $10,000/$100,000 = $2,500. However, you only paid $1,500 of tax on passive income and are therefore limited to $1,500 of passive foreign tax credit, with $0 carried forward.

Combining the two you get a total foreign tax credit on only $7,750 ($6,250 + $1,500). Because you were required to separate the income and tax into separate buckets, you are limited to $7,750 of foreign tax credit compared to what you would have received if you were able to aggregate, $8,750. The extra $1,000 is carried forward for up to ten years. Instead of having a carryover of $2,750, your carryover is $3,750.

If you are unable to fully use the entire amount of foreign tax paid as a credit in the current year, you are able to carry back the excess one year and forward 10 years, for a total of 12 years (including the current year). If you are amending last year's return by carrying back the credit, you will need to complete Amended US Individual Income Tax Return (Form 1040X) and attach the revised Form 1116. When applying the tax credit, you must first use all of the current year's tax, and then use the credits in the order they were incurred (oldest first).

Proper calculation of the foreign tax credit is very complex; do not try to compute the credit by hand. As a matter of fact, some tax software programs do not properly calculate the credit or keep track of carry forwards.

Note: You can choose to take the taxes as either a deduction or a credit, but not both. Think about what should happen if you are going along for three years and always choosing to take the credit and you have had a carry forward each year. In year four, you choose to take the deduction. What should happen with your tax credit carry forwards? Should they simply carry on as if nothing happened? Well, the answer is that you have to calculate the foreign tax credit separately, as if you had chosen the credit and you would lose the benefit of any excess credit you would have otherwise been entitled to. The following is the example from Publication 514.

- In 2008, you paid foreign taxes of $600 on general limitation income. You have a foreign tax credit carryover of $200 from the same category from 2010. For 2011, your foreign tax credit limit is $700.

    If you choose to claim a credit for your foreign taxes in 2011, you would be allowed a credit of $700, consisting of $600 paid in 2011 and $100 carried over from 2010. You will have a credit carryover to 2012 of $100, which is your unused 2010 foreign tax credit carryover.

    If you choose to deduct your foreign taxes in 2008, your deduction will be limited to $600, which is the amount of taxes paid in 2008. You are not allowed a deduction for any part of the carryover from 2007. However, you must treat $100 of the credit carryover as used in 2008, because you have an unused credit limit of $100 ($700 limit minus $600 of foreign taxes paid in 2008). This reduces your carryover to later years.

While the IRS does adequately explain how this whole thing works; no one would ever choose to take the deduction in this scenario. In real life, this would not be much of a concern because the only time you would choose to take the deduction is when you have a foreign tax that you have no hope of utilizing before it expires. So, while there might be an exception that we can't think of, in general you would choose to deduct only when you were not able to take all of the credit, let alone use up carryovers.

There is a *de minimis* exception to calculating the limits on each foreign income category. If your creditable foreign taxes are $300 ($600 married filing joint) or less and if you meet the following conditions, you can claim the taxes directly on page two (line 47 of the 2011 Form 1040) of your tax return without completing Form 1116:

- All foreign income qualifies as "passive" income

- All the income and any foreign taxes paid are reported to you on a qualified payee statement such as Form 1099 (Miscellaneous Income) or Form K-1 (Partner's Share of Income, Deductions, Credits, etc.). (**Note:** Canadian T slips and NR slips do not count as qualified payee statements.)

An election must be made to take advantage of this benefit. If you make the election, you cannot carryover any other credits to the year the election was made. You are required to reduce the taxes available for credit by any amount you would have entered on line 12 of Form 1116.

The foreign tax credit can be further limited if your foreign earned income is excluded from income using the "foreign earned income exclusion." The foreign income exclusion allows US taxpayers working in a foreign country to exclude up to $95,100 (in 2012) of foreign earned income. Earned income can be either wages or self-employment income and even some housing expenses. Even though this is foreign income and you did pay foreign tax, a foreign tax credit cannot be taken on this income if you choose to exclude the income. This makes sense since because by excluding the income, you are not paying US tax on the income and you therefore do not have a double-tax situation. (The foreign earned income exclusion is talked about in more detail in Chapter 2.)

4. Alternative Minimum Tax (AMT)

The US has an Alternative Minimum Tax (AMT) similar to the one in Canada. As part of computing your AMT in the US, you must complete a second Form 1116 to determine the amount of credit and carry forwards for AMT purposes. The *American Jobs Act* also allows for the foreign tax credit calculated under AMT to offset up to 100 percent of the foreign taxes. Previously, foreign tax credit under AMT was limited to 90 percent.

Although the AMT foreign tax credit can now be 100 percent, you will almost always have different amounts to carryover for AMT purposes than you will have for regular tax purposes. For this reason, and for many other reasons, preparing a tax return by hand is foolish, both in terms of the time it would take and that there are so many circular calculations to be made.

Note: The effect of "Foreign Earned Income" on the foreign tax credit can be further limited if your foreign earned income is excluded from income using the "foreign earned income exclusion." The foreign income exclusion allows US taxpayers working in a foreign country to "exclude" up to $95,100 of foreign earned income in 2012. Earned income can be either wages or self-employment income. Even though this is foreign income and you did pay foreign tax, a foreign tax credit cannot be taken on this income if you choose to exclude the income. This makes sense since by excluding the income, you are not paying US tax on the income and therefore do not have double-tax situation.

6

Registered Retirement Plans, Pensions, and Social Security

In this chapter, we will discuss how the US taxes the following types of accounts:

- Registered Retirement Savings Plan (RRSP)
- Registered Retirement Income Fund (RRIF)
- Locked-In Retirement Account (LIRA)
- Registered Education Savings Plan (RESP)
- Tax-Free Savings Account (TFSA)
- Registered Disability Savings Plan (RDSP)
- Individual, company, and government pension plans
- Canadian Pension Plan (CPP)
- Quebec Pension Plan (QPP)
- Old Age Security (OAS)
- US Social Security

1. Registered Retirement Plans

The US has certain types of pension plans that allow the deferral of interest, dividends, and capital gains earned inside the plan. The treatment of these US plans is very similar to Canadian RRSPs and other registered retirement plans in Canada; tax is deferred until you actually distribute the money. Tax-deferred US pension plans are referred to as "qualified plans" because they qualify for tax-free treatment by satisfying a myriad of tax and labor-law issues. Canadian RRSPs and other Canadian registered plans are not, and cannot be, qualified plans as defined by US tax law, which requires qualified plans to be created and organized in the US. Thus, income earned in an RRSP or other Canadian registered plan cannot be tax deferred or tax exempt in the US because the Canadian plans do not meet the requirements under US tax law.

So how does the IRS view Canadian registered savings plans? Article XVIII(7) of the Treaty allows for the deferral of Registered Savings Plans (RSPs). While the Treaty does not define what an RSP is, the Diplomatic Notes of the Fifth Protocol state that RSPs are registered retirement savings plans, deferred profit sharing plans, and registered retirement income funds.

Note: Nowhere does the Treaty or the IRS mention locked-in retirement accounts (LIRAs), locked-in retirement income funds (LRIFs), locked-in funds (LIF), etc., but we believe these accounts fall within the meaning of the law.

Because Canadian retirement plans do not meet the requirements of US qualified plans, they cannot be tax deferred and are therefore taxed like a non-qualified (non-registered) account. This means that they are taxed the same as any other non-registered account such as your bank or brokerage account would be taxed. However, the Treaty allows for relief from current taxation by electing under the Treaty, to defer taxation of any income earned in an RRSP (and the other accounts mentioned earlier) interest, dividends, and capital gains until the money is withdrawn. In other words, the accounts continue to be tax deferred, just like they are in Canada.

1.1. Deferral

In 1995, Article XVIII(7) was added to the Treaty to give a US citizen or resident alien the option to elect to defer the tax on the income earned and accrued in certain Canadian retirement plans until the monies were distributed. The article was put in place to address the mismatch between the timing of tax for Canada and the US, which would likely result in double taxation when the money was withdrawn.

Note: Some advisors believe that all US citizens and resident aliens owning these plans are obligated to report their clients' interests using Annual Return to Report Transactions with Foreign Trusts and Receipt of Certain Foreign Gifts (Form 3520), and Annual Information Return of Foreign Trust with a US Owner (Form 3520-A). This is not correct; the IRS has issued statements notifying taxpayers that those forms are not required. In fact, the instructions to US Information Return for Beneficiaries of Certain Canadian Registered Retirement Plans (Form 8891) states "... annuitants and beneficiaries who are required to file Form 8891 will not be required to file Form 3520 ..."

Normally the Treaty-Based Return Position Disclosure Under Section 6114 or 7701(b) (Form 8833) must be filed whenever you are taking advantage of the Treaty, but the IRS has in the Form 8891 the election and therefore, Form 8833 is not needed and should not be used when making the election to defer the earnings on your RRSPs and related accounts. A separate Form 8891 is required to be filed for each RRSP account (and other the eligible plans listed earlier) that is owned by a US citizen or resident alien. The Form must be filed annually and attached to your tax return when filed. (**Note:** You must file Form 8891 to make the Treaty election. No form, no election!)

Once this election is made, the election cannot be changed in any subsequent year. In other words, you cannot choose to defer income and then choose to pay tax in a subsequent year; an election to defer tax on unearned and undistributed income is a permanent and irrevocable election as long as the accounts exist. Without making this election, all income earned in a Canadian RRSP (and related accounts), whether or not it is distributed, is subject to US tax in the year the income was earned.

1.2 Distributions

When a distribution is made from an RRSP, you must report the total amount and the taxable amount of the distribution on Form 8891. Canadian withholding tax is imposed on distributions from the plan, and a foreign tax credit may be available to offset US tax that is imposed. While the total amount is easy enough to figure out, the taxable portion is more of a challenge.

From the US perspective, any Canadian retirement plan account is treated just like any other brokerage or investment account, except for the ability to elect to defer the income using Form 8891 for eligible plans. This is an important distinction because, when monies are withdrawn from an eligible plan account, the amount that was originally invested (the principal) will not be subject to US income tax. If you are a Canadian (but not US citizen) who is now a US resident taxpayer, the amount that was contributed, as well as any interest, dividends, and realized capital gains accrued up until the date you became a US taxpayer (typically the day of entry into the US), is considered principal (cost basis) for US tax purposes. What is not considered part of your principal is the unrealized capital gain at the date of entry. For a US citizen or a green card holder who has been a resident in Canada, only your contributions are considered principal.

If you live in a state that has an income tax, state income tax may be due on the income earned on an RRSP every year, regardless of whether you have filed the election with your federal tax return. The reason for this is that states are not party to the treaty or its elections.

Interestingly, in April of 2003, California made it clear when it issued a statement stating that it does not permit the deferral of earnings in Canadian retirement plans. This means that all California residents are required to include income from their RRSPs in their California taxable income each year. Fortunately, some state tax systems (e.g., Arizona) complement the federal tax system and allow the deferral. Also, certain states allow for offsetting the foreign tax credit for the Canadian federal and provincial taxes paid, and other states may allow for an offsetting credit for just the provincial taxes paid. These are good reasons to make sure you know how the RRSP (and related accounts) will be taxed and how foreign tax credits will be handled in the state you live.

Note: The description of taxation on withdrawal of your RRSPs is our interpretation of the law. Based on a sampling from our colleagues, it is the majority opinion, but in no way is it a unanimous opinion. Some cross-border tax experts believe that you have no principal (cost basis) in your RRSP and upon withdrawal the proceeds will be 100 percent taxable in the US. A discussion of the technical issues involved in this disagreement is beyond the scope of this book. However, here is how we look at it. We have a legitimate professional disagreement, we are in the majority, and when in doubt take the position that benefits the client.

From a Canadian perspective, there are two types of distributions — lump-sum and periodic. The only thing the Treaty says about this issue is that periodic distributions are taxed at a 15 percent withholding tax rate. In Canada, the default withholding rate (unless reduced by the Treaty) is 25 percent. The Treaty does not define either lump-sum or periodic, so all we know from the Treaty is that lump-sum payments will have a 25 percent withholding tax applied and periodic payments will have 15 percent applied. However, we can go to the *Income Tax Conventions Interpretation Act* for the definitions. The definition of lump-sum is any payment that is not a periodic payment. The definition of a periodic payment is the amount that would be the greater of —

- twice the amount of the required minimum payment; and

- 10 percent of the fair market value of the property at the beginning of the year.

1.3 Planning

In planning for what to do with your RRSPs (and related accounts) as a US tax resident, there are basically three options:

- You can make the election on Form 8891 to defer the tax and pay tax on the accumulated income when distributed.

- You can report the income each year.

- You can withdraw the funds entirely.

There is one additional option that many US taxpayers with RRSPs are unknowingly choosing — doing nothing and assuming that there is no tax on their RRSPs in the US and no reporting requirements in the US. This can be a very costly option that could result in unnecessary tax, penalties, and interest owing for failure to report the income and report the accounts. In some cases, a request for relief can be made through a request for a private letter ruling. The relief may sometimes be granted if the taxpayer acted reasonably and in good faith, and the government's grant of the relief would not prejudice the government's interests. The request for relief is a long and costly process that you should try to avoid, if at all possible.

Caution: What you think you know about the taxation of RRSPs and RRIFs is probably wrong. The reason for this is that what you know or have been told is most likely based on the laws as if you were a Canadian resident. As we discussed in Chapter 4, the laws that apply to nonresidents of Canada are different.

As a US resident taxpayer who exited Canada with RRSPs, we recommend that you determine your cost basis as of the date of exit. For Canadian purposes, the cost basis is of no concern for you because the entire account is tax deferred and becomes taxable when distributed. However, as mentioned earlier, you are not taxed on your cost basis, which is the amount you contributed to an RRSP, plus any interest, dividends, and realized capital gains, up until the date you exited Canada.

Note: The method to calculate of cost basis for a US citizen is different that the method used for non-US citizens; read carefully to make sure you are using the correct method.

The first option we mentioned is to make the election to defer the tax until the money is withdrawn. If you choose to do this, you will need to consider both the Canadian and US tax perspectives. Canada will continue to defer the tax until the money is withdrawn, then tax 100 percent of the distribution when it is paid out; the default withholding rate of 25 percent for lump-sum payments.

There are two things you need to know regarding your RRSP and RRIF withdrawals. First, you cannot make periodic distributions from an RRSP, regardless of the amount withdrawn. You must convert your RRSP to an RRIF in order to make periodic payments. Second, you can convert your RRSP to a RRIF at any time. The catch is that you must begin periodic payments in the year you convert.

On occasion, a financial institution will withhold 25 percent even though you do everything right and 15 percent tax rate should have been withheld. In that case, you will need to file a Application by a Nonresident of Canada for a Reduction in the Amount of Nonresident Tax Required to be Withheld (Form NR5) with the CRA to request the lower withholding; once approved the CRA will send you a refund check for the difference.

As you can see from Table 6, the withdrawal percentage is less than 5 percent until you reach age 70. Therefore, if you want to withdraw the maximum amount at the 15 percent withholding rate, 10 percent will be the amount you can withdraw each year until you are age 71 and older. At age 71, twice the annual percentage will be 14.76 percent (7.38 x 2) and since it is greater than 10 percent, you can withdraw this amount at the 15 percent withholding rate. Be careful to round down and not up when calculating the amount of the distribution qualifying as a periodic distribution; going over by $1 makes the entire distribution a lump-sum and subject to 25 percent withholding.

Table 6
RRIF MINIMUM WITHDRAWALS BY AGE

Age as of Jan 1	Minimum Withdrawal	Age as of Jan 1	Minimum Withdrawal	Age as of Jan 1	Minimum Withdrawal
1	1.12%	33	1.75%	65	4.00%
2	1.14%	34	1.79%	66	4.17%
3	1.15%	35	1.82%	67	4.35%
4	1.16%	36	1.85%	68	4.55%
5	1.18%	37	1.89%	69	4.76%
6	1.19%	38	1.92%	70	5.00%
7	1.20%	39	1.96%	71	7.38%
8	1.22%	40	2.00%	72	7.48%
9	1.23%	41	2.04%	73	7.59%
10	1.25%	42	2.08%	74	7.71%
11	1.27%	43	2.13%	75	7.85%
12	1.28%	44	2.17%	76	7.99%
13	1.30%	45	2.22%	77	8.15%
14	1.32%	46	2.27%	78	8.33%
15	1.33%	47	2.33%	79	8.53%
16	1.35%	48	2.38%	80	8.75%
17	1.37%	49	2.44%	81	8.99%
18	1.39%	50	2.50%	82	9.27%
19	1.41%	51	2.56%	83	9.58%

20	1.43%	52	2.63%	84	9.93%
21	1.45%	53	2.70%	85	10.33%
22	1.47%	54	2.78%	86	10.79%
23	1.49%	55	2.86%	87	11.33%
24	1.52%	56	2.94%	88	11.96%
25	1.54%	57	3.03%	89	12.71%
26	1.56%	58	3.13%	90	13.62%
27	1.59%	59	3.23%	91	14.73%
28	1.61%	60	3.33%	92	16.12%
29	1.64%	61	3.45%	93	17.92%
30	1.67%	62	3.57%	94	20.00%
31	1.69%	63	3.70%	95+	20.00%
32	1.72%	64	3.85%		

You may run into Canadian brokers who are unwilling to hold an RRSP for nonresidents of Canada. This is because there are rules that are set out by the US Securities and Exchange Commission (SEC) restricting securities brokers and dealers to provide services only to residents of their own country. The SEC recognized that these rules caused an undue hardship on US residents who hold RRSP accounts and issued an order to offer reprieve to this problem. If you have a broker or dealer that is unwilling to hold RRSP assets for you as a US resident taxpayer, you should refer the broker or dealer to the SEC's website for Release No. 34-42906; International Series Release No. 1227 at www.sec.gov/rules/other/34-42906.htm.

As part of the IRS regulations under the *Foreign Account Tax Compliance Act* (FATCA), US taxpayers with specific types and amounts of foreign financial assets or financial accounts, which include all Canadian retirement plan accounts, must file an information disclosure, IRS Statement of Specified Foreign Financial Assets (Form 8938) each tax year. Reporting threshold amounts vary according to filing status. Failure to file can subject a taxpayer to a US$10,000 penalty as well as other sanctions.

In addition, any resident taxpayer who owns accounts, including Canadian retirement accounts, in countries outside of the US, is required to file a Report of Foreign Bank and Financial Accounts (Form TD F 90-22.1) with the Department of the Treasury in each year that the total of all foreign accounts exceeds US$10,000, at any time during the year. There are two key points here; $10,000 in aggregate and at any time during the year. If you have five accounts, none of which exceed $10,000 on its own, but in total exceed $10,000, you must file Form TD F 90-22.1 for each account. The other point is that the total of your accounts may not typically exceed $10,000, but they exceed $10,000, even for a moment, you must file Form TD F 90-22.1 for all foreign accounts. The most frequent reason for accounts spiking for short periods of time is when a house is sold; the proceeds come to you and you turnaround and write a check for a new home.

As pointed out in the book *The Border Guide: A Guide to Living, Working and Investing Across the Border*, written by Robert Keats, there are many reasons why it may be wise to cash out your RRSPs (and related accounts) once you are in the US. There are a number of risks that arise that were not present when you were a Canadian resident, assuming you are not a US citizen. We will highlight some of the risks here, but I suggest you read *The Border Guide* for more details. The major risks include the following:

- Tax compliance is more complicated and therefore costly.

- The additional complexity creates a risk that a form is not filed or filed properly, leaving you open to potentially large penalties.

- You have exposure to currency exchange risk. While you are holding on to your accounts so that you can defer the tax to a later date, while you are holding those accounts, you run the risk of the Canadian dollar falling relative to the US dollar. The currency market is not a free market, so regardless of how smart you think you are, or your advisor is, you have no idea what currency prices will do because the government could step in at any time and cause their currency to go higher or lower depending on what objective they are trying to reach. Why take the risk?

- If you die still owning an RRSP or similar account, you could be subject to double tax. The US estate tax exemption is scheduled to drop to $1,000,000 per person, indexed for inflation (approximately $1,300,000 after inflation). This means that if your net worth is greater than approximately $1.3 million, you will be subject to US estate tax. While the Treaty has a provision that generally provides for a foreign tax credit on taxes due at death, there is one exception; the Canadian tax must be due to capital gains. Canadian tax on your RRSP is at ordinary rates and is not classified as a capital gain, and therefore no foreign tax credit is allowed.

- If you die still owning an RRSP you could be subject to double tax in the US. If you are subject to US estate tax, discussed above, the US will impose an estate tax at death and the beneficiary will have to pay income tax when the money is withdrawn (assuming the beneficiary is a US taxpayer). This is double tax. Add the Canadian tax above and you have triple tax. If your net worth is large enough to be subject to US estate tax, this should be reason enough to cash out your RRSP type accounts.

- States like California will tax your RRSP each year even if you made the election to defer per the Treaty.

- Canadian mutual funds are the most expensive in the world. Canadian mutual funds are generally twice as expensive as the equivalent US funds. So if you are paying 1 percent more a year in mutual fund expenses, in ten years you would exceed (with compounding) the 10 percent saving in the difference in the lump-sum and periodic withdrawal strategies.

In summary, the decision to hold onto your tax-deferred accounts and defer paying taxes for as long as possible is not clear cut, and possibly the wrong thing to do once you move to the US. When you are living in Canada (assuming you are not a US citizen), the only factor to consider is whether you should pay tax now or pay later. As we all know, the answer to that question will almost always be to wait as long as possible. However, when you move across the border, the issues become more numerous and more serious. You need to break away from you old way of thinking and address the very real risks of leaving your RRSP in Canada, as a US resident.

1.4 How the taxes work

To determine the US tax on distributions from your registered retirement accounts, you first must determine your cost basis (principal) for US purposes. We discussed this in section 1.2, but it is the fair market value of the accounts, less any unrealized capital gains, on the date you became a US taxpayer. The amount of US income you would have to report from any distribution is equal to percentage of the account withdrawn (e.g., 100 percent, 10 percent) times the fair market value of the account on the date of the distribution, less your US cost basis. If you are a US citizen that has been living in Canada and contributing to an RRSP, your cost basis will generally be limited to the amount of your contributions. However, this could be different because the Treaty was amended a few years ago to allow for RRSP contributions to be deductible on your US tax return, with some limitations. If you deducted contributions to your RRSP on your US return, those contributions do not increase your cost basis. Here is an example:

- You moved to the US on January 1, 2010, and the value of your RRSP on that date was $300,000. You had $20,000 of unrealized capital gains in your account as of that date. This means that your US cost basis is $280,000. If you were to cash out your RRSP on that day, you would have had to report $20,000 of income on your US return. However, if you had a distribution of 10 percent of your account value on that date, you would have to report 10 percent of $20,000, or $2,000. Another way of looking at this is that you used up $18,000 of your US cost basis, therefore your cost basis going forward is reduced from $280,000 to $262,000.

Note: In states that allow for the deferral of tax on your RRSP type accounts (e.g., Arizona), your US and Arizona cost basis is the same and there is nothing special you need to do. However, if you live in a state that does not allow for the deferral (e.g., California), your cost basis will increase, for California but not US purposes, each year you pay California tax. This means that you will need to keep two sets of cost basis records.

The withholding taxes that are paid to Canada are eligible as a foreign tax credit in the US. These taxes can only be used to the extent that there is foreign source income, and to be more specific, passive foreign source income, which is generally all income except income from employment and company or government pension related earnings. The distributions that you receive from your RRSPs are deemed to be passive foreign source income, but only to the extent that the distributions are taxable in the US. The credit is calculated on the Form 1116 (Foreign Tax Credit) and can be complicated, but in its most simple form, it is a credit against your US taxes using a percentage allocation based on a ratio of foreign source income to worldwide income. (See Chapter 5 for a more thorough discussion of foreign tax credits.)

The second option is to pay the tax each year. Instead of deferring the income by making the election on Form 8891, you would instead report and pay tax on any interest, dividend, and capital gain income earned each tax year. From a US tax perspective, this option could be appealing: The income is taxed based on the character of the income. Interest income is taxed at a taxpayer's ordinary income tax rates, and dividends and capital gains are generally taxed at 15 percent (2012). Compare this to how your income is taxed if you decide to defer the tax: The income accrued in the account is taxed when distributed, and it is taxed at your higher ordinary income tax rates. There is no tax break from the type of income that generated the earnings in the account. However, there is the problem of the mismatch of when the income is taxed by Canada, potentially resulting in double taxation. Because Canada will tax you when distributions are made and the US will tax you as income is earned (assuming you do not elect to defer). Only in very rare circumstances would this option make sense.

As a US tax resident, you have a third option which is to take a lump-sum withdrawal from your RRSP. To do this, all of the positions would be liquidated in the Canadian retirement plan and the funds would be withdrawn in a one-time lump-sum distribution and transferred into a US bank or brokerage account. You would incur a 25 percent withholding tax payable to CRA upon withdrawal. If you elected to defer your taxes on Form 8891, you will be taxed in the US when the money is withdrawn, but only on the earnings in the account since the date you exited Canada plus any unrealized earnings on investments in the account at your exit date, and at your ordinary tax rates.

Whenever you pay more Canadian tax than US tax, you will have unused credits that can be carried forward for up to 10 future years, and back 1 year (for a total of 12 years, including the current year), as necessary. By investing some or all of your proceeds into foreign securities that produce foreign passive income, it may be possible to use your unused credits to fully offset the taxes on your investment earnings from foreign passive investments for years to come.

Caution: Be sure to work with investment professionals who know how to manage a portfolio designed to utilize foreign tax credits because generating foreign passive income is not as easy as it sounds. The challenges to generating foreign passive income include the following:

- You cannot generally invest in foreign securities as a nonresident because of securities laws.

- Even if you were to find a firm that would allow you to invest in foreign securities, you have to be concerned with the potentially high costs, lack of diversification, currency risk, and foreign tax being withheld on those earnings (analogous to taking two steps forward and one step back).

- US mutual funds that invest in foreign securities will solve most of these problems but have one critical flaw; the income is not considered foreign because the mutual fund takes the foreign tax credit at the fund level. This means that the investor cannot claim the income as foreign and take the credit for it; otherwise, a foreign tax credit would have been taken twice on the same income.

Because the Canadian tax paid usually exceeds the US tax, you may end up with excess foreign tax credits available to carry forward and apply to other foreign passive taxable income over the next 11 years. It is important to mention that when you take a lump-sum withdrawal, your marginal US tax rate may increase because of the additional income. You should take this into consideration when determining a strategy for liquidating your RRSPs.

There are currently six provinces that allow nonresident Canadians to unlock their LIRAs: British Columbia, Alberta, Saskatchewan, Ontario, Quebec, and New Brunswick. If you have a LIRA in these provinces you can request to unlock your LIRA by providing evidence that you are a nonresident of Canada, specifically in the form of a confirmation from CRA that you are a nonresident. The CRA written confirmation can be obtained by filing the Determination of Residency Status (Form NR73). It usually takes about eight weeks to receive an answer.

There is also relief for LIRAs held by former employees of federally regulated industries, such as airlines, railroads, and communications companies. To qualify, the employees must be currently a nonresident of Canada and have been a nonresident for at least two years.

Note: Once the NR73 is approved and the CRA certifies that you are a nonresident, you can break the lock. In most cases, you cannot make a partial withdrawal of the LIRA; you must make a full withdrawal immediately.

When dealing with RRSPs and LIRAs as a nonresident of Canada, we recommend that you seek the advice of an experienced and qualified cross-border professional.

Many Canadians have locked-in retirement accounts (LIRAs) that were created through an employment-pension plan regulated at the provincial level. All provinces and territories have legislation where employer-funded pension plans can be locked until retirement age, even after an employee has left the company. In 2000, the CRA recognized that an undue hardship was being imposed on nonresident Canadians who held locked-in accounts, including LIRAs and LRIFs (hereinafter collectively referred to as "LIRAs"). The hardship was a result of the potential double taxation resulting from a timing mismatch between the Canadian tax system and other countries' tax systems. As a result of lobbying from the CRA and other countries, many provinces provided relief for nonresident LIRA owners.

1.5 Other types of accounts

Unfortunately, for other types of Canadian retirement plans, such as tax-free savings accounts (TFSAs), registered education savings plans (RESPs), and registered disability savings plans (RDSPs), the simplified reporting requirements using Form 8891 do not apply. For these non-eligible plans, there is a significant risk of double taxation. The election to defer is not permitted, and for US resident aliens or citizens who own these types of plans, Annual Return to Report Transactions with Foreign Trusts and Receipt of Certain Foreign Gifts (Form 3520) and/or Annual Information Return of Foreign Trust with a US Owner (Form 3520-A) must be filed every year for RESPs and RDSPs, but apparently not for TFSAs. These burdensome filing requirements are just the beginning; what's worse is that the income earned in these types of plans is taxable in the US in the tax year for which the income is earned, even if the income is not distributed. The same income that is taxable in the US is not subject to Canadian tax until distributed from the plan. The timing mismatch between the two countries will most likely cause the individual to suffer double taxation.

Don't forget that in addition to potentially having to file Forms 3520 and 3520-A, you are definitely required to file Forms TD F 90-22.1 and 8938 if the total of all of your foreign accounts exceed $10,000 at any point during the year.

For those taxpayers who have accounts that cannot be deferred (e.g., TFSAs, RESPs, RDSPs, you should seriously consider the option of taking the lump-sum withdrawal to minimize the double taxation issue as well as the onerous reporting requirements.

2. Pensions

In this context, the term pension means a retirement benefit provided by an employer (including the government) to an employee for services provided to the employer over a period of years. This does not include Canadian Pension Plan or Quebec Pension Plan; these plans are a form of social security and are discussed in section **3.**

For years, pensions were treated very similar to RRSPs in that they had a US cost basis, but about a decade ago the law was changed and a new section to the Internal Revenue Code (IRC) was added. That section is 72(w). In general, section 72 lays out the laws surrounding annuities. Below is a quote from IRC 72(w) Application of Basis Rules to Nonresident Aliens:

"In general — notwithstanding any other provision of this section, for purposes of determining the portion of any distribution which is includable in gross income of a distributee who is a citizen or resident of the United States, the investment in the contract shall not include any applicable nontaxable contributions or applicable nontaxable earnings."

What this is saying in English is that there is no US cost basis and therefore 100 percent of the pension is taxable in the US

Pensions are classified as general limitation income for foreign tax credit purposes. This means that you will have two separate foreign tax credit forms (Form 1116) and because they are different types of foreign income, they cannot be used to help offset the other's foreign tax credits. Withholding on pensions or annuities is 15 percent regardless of the size of the pension or annuity; we have had clients who have had pensions that paid them more than a million dollars per year and they still had 15 percent withheld.

3. Social Security

As a US tax resident, you are entitled to receive the benefits that you earned through the Canadian Pension Plan (CPP) or Quebec Pension Plan (QPP) and Old Age Security (OAS) systems while you were a Canadian resident, there are no unique requirements for eligibility because you are now a nonresident of Canada.

There are unique tax advantages for you as a nonresident of Canada verses being a Canadian resident when it comes to receiving benefits from CPP or QPP and OAS. As a US resident, your CPP or QPP and OAS are taxed only in the US and no longer taxed in Canada. As a US resident, you will receive the full benefit payment, without withholding and without any further tax reporting requirements. As a US resident, you are no longer subject to the OAS claw-back rules and you will receive your benefit regardless of your income. This is an ironic benefit for Canadians who leave Canada — it took you many years of living in Canada to earn the OAS benefits, but if you stayed in Canada, the benefits would have been taken away from you. Only by leaving Canada can many people actually receive their OAS benefits.

Note: Depending on how long you lived in Canada prior to leaving, you may receive full, partial, or no OAS benefits. To receive full benefits, you must have lived in Canada at least 20 years after the age of 18. To receive partial benefits, you must have lived in Canada at least 10 years after the age of 18. Less than 10 in Canada after the age of 18 and you are not eligible for benefits. Eligibility for CPP or QPP is the same as it is if you were still a resident of Canada, it is based on years of work and payment into the system.

Instead of being taxed in Canada, the income from CPP or QPP and OAS is taxed in the US in the same way that US taxpayers report social security income. The benefits are generally not taxable if your income (including the CPP or QPP and OAS) is less than US$25,000 if you are single, or US$32,000 for a married couple. If your income exceeds US$34,000 for singles (or $44,000 for a married couple), then 85 percent of your benefit is subject to income tax, and 15 percent is tax free. If you fall somewhere between the upper and lower limits, then your percentage of taxable benefits varies between 0 percent and 85 percent.

3.1 The Windfall Elimination Provision

While the Windfall Elimination Provision (WEP) is not a tax issue, it is an area of concern and confusion so we want to spend some time discussing the basics. For more information on WEP you can go to the Social Security Administration website at www.ssa.gov and read the book *The Border Guide*, where substantially more time is devoted to this subject.

WEP may apply whenever you worked in a job that you earned foreign social security benefits (CPP or QPP), without paying US social security taxes. If the WEP applies to you, your benefits can be reduced by as much as 60 percent. The good news is that the WEP rules don't apply to you because of the Canada-US Agreement on Social Security. The bad news is that the Social Security Administration employees have little to no training on this subject. We have taken on a couple of these cases in the past and have won at the internal appeals level, but the results of those cases never make it into the training. The real problem is that the cost of fighting is greater than the benefit lost, so it is not cost effective to fight the issue.

If the Social Security Administration is telling you that you are subject to the WEP, our suggestion is to read the Canada-US Agreement on Social Security carefully and appeal your own case. Information can be found at Service Canada website www.servicecanada.gc.ca. The Agreement can be found at www.socialsecurity.gov/international/Agreement_Texts/canada.html.

7

Investments

While investing in the US is fundamentally the same as investing in Canada, there are many differences that you should become familiar with. For starters, the US is much larger in terms of size and investment types. Many of the different investment types provide tax advantages that are not available in Canada.

In addition to listing some of the more common investment options and their tax characteristics, we will talk briefly about some of the differences in fees, securities laws, how investment advice is provided in the US, which is significantly different than in Canada.

1. Securities Law

From a regulatory point of view, one of the big differences between the US and Canada is the fact that the US has a national regulatory system, whereas in Canada, securities regulation is a provincial matter. While the US does have the Securities and Exchange Commission (SEC) to oversee securities regulation, some advisors may not be regulated by the SEC. If an advisor is considered a small advisor, meaning that the advisor has $50 million or less of assets under his or her management, the state or states that he or she works in will oversee the advisor's activity. The point of mentioning this is to make you aware that even though we have a national regulator, not all advisors have the same supervision. We cannot say which is better; we can only point out that they may be different. All SEC registered advisors are subject to the same rules, but the state rules may vary from the SEC and from each other.

Caution: When comparing advisors, beware that from a regulatory point of view, you may not be comparing apples to apples. Be sure to ask whether the advisor is an SEC registered advisor or not.

One question we get a lot that has to do with securities law is whether you, as a nonresident of Canada and resident of the US, can leave your registered and nonregistered accounts in Canada. The Canadian and American securities regulators were established, primarily to protect its residents from abusive and fraudulent sales practices. As long as you are a resident, the government can try to protect your regulations and sanctions of advisors doing business in their country. However, if you are in one country and your investment accounts are in the other country, it becomes much more difficult to protect you.

For years, Canadian advisors were prohibited from advising on any securities people left in Canada. What was happening was that Canadians were leaving their registered accounts (e.g., RRSPs and RRIFs) in Canada after they had moved to the US and they were stuck in the predicament of having to choose between lying to their advisor, telling the truth and having the account frozen (since the advisor could not advise a nonresident), or cash their registered accounts, pay the tax, and bring them to the US. Because of this, the securities regulators agreed to make an exception for Canadians that leave their registered accounts in Canada.

No exception was made for nonregistered accounts such as your typical brokerage account. To date there is still no exception to this rule. If you choose to leave your brokerage account in Canada, it will be frozen. While you can direct your advisor to sell, the advisor cannot buy securities. This rule does not apply to bank accounts such as checkings, savings, or Guaranteed Investment Certificates (GICs), because these accounts are not securities.

2. Mutual Funds

For many years, Canadian mutual funds have been ranked the most expensive in the world. Not one of the most expensive, the most expensive mutual funds in the world. In 2009, Morningstar, Inc., a leading provider of independent investment research in North America, Europe, Australia, and Asia, produced a research report titled Morningstar Global Fund Investor Experience in May of 2009. The research showed that Canadian mutual funds are about twice as expensive as the equivalent US mutual funds. Here is the link to the full report: corporate.morningstar.com/us/documents/ResearchPapers/MRGFI.pdf. Table 7 is a summary of the expenses.

Table 7
SUMMARY OF EXPENSES

Typical Canadian Mutual Fund Investor	Typical US Mutual Fund Investor	Difference Per Year
Fixed Income Fund – 1.25% to 1.49% per year	Fixed Income Fund – less than .75% per year	.5% to .75% (67% to 100% higher)
Equity Fund – 2% to 2.5% per year	Equity Fund – less than 1% per year	1% to 1.5% (100% to 150% higher)

The report only shows the averages, it does not point out that the US has many more low-cost options than Canada. Index funds and exchange traded funds (ETFs) have very low expenses. For example, Vanguard Funds has an equity index fund that cost as little as 0.05 percent per year. Agreed that this example is extreme, but it is an example of how inexpensive mutual funds can be in the US. If you use index funds or ETFs, you can expect the annual expenses to be about half of the average, or about 0.5 percent per year. While index funds and ETFs are gaining in popularity in Canada, there are still fewer options than in the US. In addition to their low costs, index funds and ETFs are more tax efficient than traditional mutual funds because of the low turnover.

The following sections discuss tax reporting of Canadian mutual funds.

2.1 Passive foreign investment company (PFIC) rules

The following is one of the more ridiculous results of a law that we have seen. In an effort to prevent abuse of foreign corporations owned by US individuals, Congress and the IRS established laws that require rather stringent reporting requirements and potentially serious tax consequences. Those rules have been interpreted as applying to Canadian mutual funds, so now all US taxpayers owning Canadian mutual funds must follow these passive foreign investment company (PFIC) rules.

A PFIC is a foreign (non-US) corporation that meets either an income or asset test. The income test is met if 75 percent or more of the foreign corporation's gross income is passive income. The asset test is met if at least 50 percent of the assets held by the foreign corporation are assets that produce passive income or that are held for the production of passive income.

Passive income is determined in accordance with the foreign personal holding company provisions, and includes interest, dividends, certain rents and royalties, annuities, capital gains from the sale or exchange of stock or securities, and foreign currency gains. There is no minimum ownership requirement in order for the PFIC rules to apply.

If you are a US taxpayer and receive income from a PFIC or recognize a gain from the sale of PFIC's shares, you are subject to a special tax and interest regime. The following are methods that may be used to determine the amount of income you will have to recognize as a result of your investment in a Canadian mutual fund.

2.1a Qualified electing fund (QEF)

A PFIC is considered a qualified electing fund if you, as a direct or indirect shareholder of the PFIC, elects to treat the PFIC as a qualified electing fund (QEF). What this means is, the PFIC is a QEF if you make the election to make it a QEF. The election must be made on the Information Return by a Shareholder of a Passive Foreign Investment Company or Qualifying Electing Fund (Form 8621). If the QEF election is made, on an annual basis, you must include in your gross income your pro-rata share of the ordinary earnings, and the net capital gain of the QEF.

In order for the QEF election to apply, the PFIC must provide its shareholders with a PFIC Annual Information Statement. This statement must contain certain information, such as the shareholder's pro-rata share of the PFIC's ordinary income and net capital gain for that taxable year, or sufficient information to enable the shareholders to calculate their pro-rata share of the PFIC's ordinary income and net capital gain for the year.

In addition, the PFIC must either obtain the permission of the IRS to be treated as a PFIC, or provide a statement indicating that it will permit its investors to inspect and copy sufficient information to confirm the PFIC's ordinary earnings and net capital gains, as determined in accordance with US income tax principles. If neither condition is met, the QEF election cannot be applied.

Note: The QEF election will not be available to US taxpayers who own shares in Canadian mutual funds because the mutual funds are not complying with the rules.

2.1b Mark-to-market election

A shareholder of a PFIC may also elect each year to recognize the gain or loss on the shares as if they had sold the PFIC shares at fair market value at the end of the taxable year. Called a "mark-to-market election," this election must also be made on Form 8621. The gain is treated as ordinary income, not a capital gain.

The mark-to-market election is only available for marketable shares. Marketable shares are shares that are regularly traded on a US securities exchange that is registered with the US Securities and Exchange Commission (SEC), or on a foreign securities exchange that is regulated or supervised by a governmental authority of the country in which the market is located, and has certain characteristics as described in the US tax code. The problem with this method is that you have no way of knowing what the mutual fund bought the securities for so you have no way of knowing what the gain would be if the securities were mark-to-market and even if you did, who is going to pay for your accountant to go through each of the potentially thousands of securities in your Canadian mutual funds?

2.1c Excess distribution

If neither a QEF election nor a mark-to-market election is made (this will be the typical scenario), or if an election is made, but not on a timely basis, the shareholders will be subject to special rules when they receive an excess distribution. An excess distribution is the part of the distribution received in the current tax year that is greater than 125 percent of the average distributions received by the shareholder during the three preceding tax years. The excess distribution is determined on a per share basis, and is allocated to each day in the shareholder's holding period of the stock.

The amount allocated to the current year is included as ordinary income in the shareholder's gross income for the current year. Any amounts allocated to prior years are subject to tax at the highest rate of tax in effect for the applicable class of taxpayer for that year, and an interest charge will be imposed with respect to the resulting tax attributable to each such other taxable year.

Here is another accounting nightmare example: Can you imagine the work involved in determining prior distributions on a per share, per day basis? What if you have held the mutual fund for 5, 10, or 15 years? The government has put you in a no-win situation — spend a fortune on tax preparation or break the law. The only viable option is to cash out all of your Canadian mutual funds, before or shortly after exiting Canada.

3. Tax Reporting Slips

Similar to the T slips you received when you were a resident of Canada and the NR slips you are (or should be) getting from Canada as a nonresident, in the US you will be issued tax slips called 1099s. These tax slips come in a number of varieties such as the following:

- Dividends and Distributions (Form1099-DIV)

- Interest Income (Form 1099-INT)

- Proceeds from Broker and Barter Exchange Transactions (Form 1099-B)

- Distributions from Pensions, Annuities, Retirement or Profit-Sharing Plans, IRAs, Insurance Contracts, etc. (Form 1099-R)

- Miscellaneous Income (Form 1099-MISC)

Most 1099 forms are required to be sent to you by January 31, except for the Form 1099-B, which must be sent by February 15. Generally speaking you will receive a 1099 (one for each type of income, from each payor) if you received interest, dividend, or royalty income of at least $10; most others types of income have a $600 threshold before 1099s are issued by a payor.

4. Taxation of Specific Types of Investments

The following sections discuss the taxation of specific types of investments such as municipal and government bonds, annuities, personal residence, and investment real estate.

4.1 Municipal bonds

Municipal bonds (also called "muni bonds") are issued by state and local (city) governments and the interest paid is generally tax free. There are three types of municipal bonds:

- Public purpose bonds
- Qualified private activity bonds
- Non-qualified private activity bonds.

Public purpose bonds are tax free at the federal level and tax free in the state of the issuer of the bond. In New York and California you can buy mutual funds that invest entirely in that state's municipal bonds. If you live in another state, you will either have to buy individual bonds or a mutual fund with municipal bonds from many states. If you invest in a mutual fund with municipal bonds from many states, the mutual fund company will provide you a breakout of the percentages for each state. You will need this breakout when preparing your tax return.

Note: Municipal bonds from Puerto Rico, Guam and the Virgin Islands are tax free at the federal level, as well as in all states.

4.2 Government bonds

The US government issues many types of bonds, some of which you can defer the interest for up to 30 years and others are free of state income tax. EE and I (inflation) savings bonds allow you to buy US savings bonds with as little as $25. The interest grows tax deferred until the bond is redeemed, or 30 years, whichever comes first. The bonds must be held for at least 12 months before they can be redeemed. If redeemed in years two through five, you will lose three months of interest.

The difference between the two types of bonds is the EE bonds pay a fixed rate of interest, whereas the I bonds pay a lower fixed rate of interest, but can pay more if inflation increases. The US government also issues Treasury bills, notes, and bonds. The only difference in the different types of treasuries are their length of maturity. Treasuries are taxable on the federal level, but are tax free at the state level.

4.3 Annuities

Annuities in the US are essentially the same as annuities in Canada, with one major exception, the earnings and growth within the annuity is tax deferred until withdrawn. When the money is withdrawn it is taxed as ordinary income, regardless of how it was earned (e.g., interest, dividends, or capital gains). With capital gain and dividend tax rates at 15%, it may be difficult for a deferred annuity to obtain better, after tax returns than a traditional investment portfolio.

If you have an estate that exceeds the exemption amount (a taxable estate), investments that have accrued, but untaxed income at the time of death will be double taxed. The phenomenon is called "income in respect of a decedent" (IRD). Other examples of IRD would include tax-deferred retirement plans such as IRAs and 401(k)s; it would even include wages that you earned but have not been paid (dying in between pay days). It is double taxed because the value of the asset would be in the deceased's estate and in the beneficiaries' income when received.

4.4 Personal residence

The definition of a principal residence is very similar to the definition in Canada; it is basically the home you spend most of your time. However, unlike Canada where you are allowed an unlimited exemption from gain on your principal residence, the US allows only $250,000 per person. You qualify for the exclusion if the place was your principal residence for at least two of the last five years. This would apply to your Canadian home as well. One big difference in the tax laws of the US and Canada as it relates to your principal residence is that in the US, you can deduct your mortgage interest and real estate taxes.

4.5 Investment real estate

While the definition of investment property in the US and Canada are essentially the same, the US tax governing real estate for investment is substantially more complex. The very first thing to consider is where you are "active" or "passive" in your real estate investment activity. While a whole chapter could be devoted to this topic, at the most basic level, the IRS uses hours and percent of time spent to determine active verses passive. Most investors will be considered passive, meaning that some or all of their losses will be able to be used in the year they occurred. If you are unable to use your current year's losses because you are considered passive and exceed the income threshold, you will accumulate those losses (carry them over to future years) until you have passive income or when you sell the asset. Note that you cannot use passive losses to offset active income.

Another couple of US tax laws that are different than Canada are the fact that you must take depreciation (capital cost allowance) each year. Canada allows you the option of taking capital cost allowance or not, but you can never incur a loss due to capital cost allowance. Most investors do not take the capital cost allowance because it is recaptured when the property is sold.

The US allows the gain from real estate to be deferred using a tax-free exchange of "like kind" property. There are specific rules that apply to the like-kind exchange, be sure to seek advice before selling your property.

Also, when you sell the property you can also choose to carry the note over a period of years. This is called an "installment sale." You only have to report the gain as a percentage of the note (and cash down payment) made. This means that you are able to defer a percentage of the tax on the gain for the duration of the note.

5. Treaty Rules That Affect Your Securities

In Canada, a principal residence is 100 percent excluded from tax. If the former (Canadian) principal residence is retained when moving to the US, the taxpayer's basis is the fair market value (FMV) on the date of exit. Any appreciation after exit from Canada will be taxable in Canada upon sale. An appraisal or broker's opinion of the home should be received around the exit date for use in determining the FMV so that when the house is eventually sold you will have an accurate and defensible cost basis number. The US does allow a foreign residence to be a principle residence.

The Treaty has a provision that governs the taxation of real property other than a principle residence. Canada will withhold on the selling price unless a Clearance Certificate is issued. Canada Revenue Agency (CRA) issues the Clearance Certificate. The intent of the Clearance Certificate is to show the CRA the approximate gain on the property. The taxpayer must supply the sales price, purchase price, improvements, and capital cost allowance (depreciation) taken (if any) so that the gain before expenses can be determined. This allows the CRA to withhold on the gain rather than the gross sales price. The taxpayer will need to file a Canadian return by April 30 of the year following the transaction to report the expenses of the sale and receive a refund of the over withholding.

Article XIII, Paragraph 4, of the Treaty governs the taxation of securities sold. Per the Treaty, securities sold in Canada are taxable only in the country of residence (i.e., the US). The nondiscrimination or "savings" clause of the Treaty prevents the reverse from being true. Because as a US citizen you are taxable on your world income, a US citizen in Canada will have to report the sale on both the US and Canadian returns. A foreign tax credit is used to prevent double taxation.

8

Common Deductions

US taxpayers are able to deduct certain expenses on their US income tax returns. Expenses can result in adjustments, deductions, exemptions, or credits, all of which are treated in different ways to reduce your US tax liability. As Canadians, you may recognize some similarities to reductions available for Canadian tax returns. Unfortunately, not all of your expenses can reduce taxable income, but the expenses that do reduce your tax or taxable income are benefits for you. Some of these beneficial expenses may not result from expenditures that you have made. In most cases, however, you actually paid out-of-pocket money for specific items that are described in the Internal Revenue Code as available to reduce your taxes. The tax benefit that you receive is often limited to a percentage of your total actual cost or has a maximum threshold.

As you go through this chapter, we have categorized the expenses based on how they are used in calculating net taxable income or the tax calculation. This chapter focuses on deductions, exemptions, and credits.

Table 8 is the format for the US Individual Income Tax Return (Form 1040).

Table 8
THE FORMAT OF THE US INDIVIDUAL INCOME TAX RETURN
(FORM 1040)

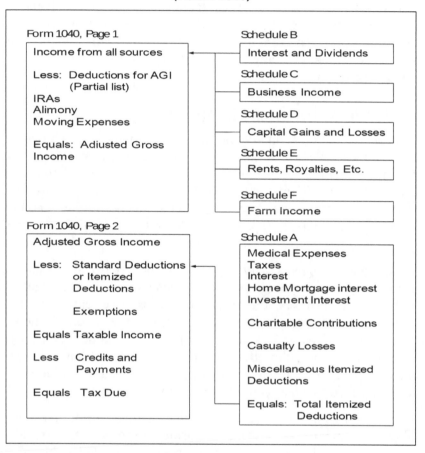

1. Above-the-Line Deductions

In determining US taxable income, there are "above-the-line deductions" and "below-the-line" deductions. So, what is the line? It is the taxpayer's Adjusted Gross Income (AGI). AGI is an important subtotal because it is used in computing the percentage limitations on itemized deductions and in other areas in the tax computation. So, not only do above-the-line deductions simply reduce taxable income, they can lower the thresholds by which other deductions are determined.

A similar calculation methodology is used for nonresident aliens filing a US Nonresident Alien Income Tax Return (Form 1040-NR). Nonresident aliens can claim deductions to figure their effectively connected taxable income. They cannot claim deductions related to income that is not connected with their US business activities. Except for personal exemptions and certain itemized deductions, a nonresident alien can only claim deductions to the extent they are connected with US income.

2. Trade or Business Expenses

You can deduct all ordinary and necessary expenses for the operation of a US trade or business operated as a sole proprietor or as the single member of a limited liability company, on Schedule C, attached to your Form 1040 or 1040-NR. If you operate a business that is organized as a corporation, a multimember limited liability company, or a partnership, separate tax returns must be filed for those entities.

Ordinary and necessary expenses include reasonable salaries paid for services, expenses for use of business property, one-half of self-employment taxes, and other business expenses customary for your type of business. It does not include charitable contributions, gifts, illegal bribes or kickbacks, or fines and penalties. Other expenses that are not allowed include political contributions or lobbying expenses, unless the lobbying expenses are used for influencing local legislation such as your city or county government.

It is sometimes difficult to determine whether or not an expenditure is deductible as a trade or business expense. The expenditure must be both "ordinary" and "necessary" to be deductible. The courts have held that an expense is necessary if a prudent businessperson would incur the same expense and the expense is appropriate and helpful in the taxpayer's business. It is ordinary if it is usual or customary in the type of business. Capital expenditures are not deductible as ordinary or necessary, but depreciation is deductible.

Allowable business expenses include legal expenses in defense of a civil or criminal claim or penalty, as long as the taxpayer can show that the claim or penalty was directly related to the trade or business; an income producing activity; or the determination, collection, or refund of a tax. Personal legal expenses are not deductible.

A bad business debt can be a deduction for Adjusted Gross Income (AGI). A bad debt results when a taxpayer sells goods or services on credit, and the accounts receivable subsequently becomes worthless. A bad debt deduction can only be taken if the income arising from the creation of the accounts receivable was included in the taxable income. A bad debt can also result from the non-repayment of a loan made by the taxpayer or from purchased debt instruments.

A nonbusiness bad debt is not a deduction for AGI but is a short-term capital loss. Loans to relatives or friends are the most common type of nonbusiness bad debt.

A bad debt can result from a deposit in an insolvent financial institution. There are specific rules if you have an ownership interest in the financial institution; however, generally, a bad debt results from this type of loss.

If you do not have a trade or business but merely have a hobby, which is an activity that may not have been engaged in for profit, you may still be able to deduct expenses, but only to the extent there is income from the hobby. How do you know if you have a hobby or a business? Generally, there is a presumptive rule that an activity is profit-seeking if it has made a profit for three of the last five years, or, if it involves horses, the activity would be a trade or business if it has made a profit for at least two of seven consecutive years. See Table 9.

There are many rules about what constitutes trade or business expenses; your tax accountant can help guide you through the rules to determine whether or not you can deduct expenses.

3. Vacation or Rental Home Expenses

If you own a home in the US and receive rental income, there are a complex set of rules that you must follow, but you are able to deduct expenses as long as they are related to the rental of the home and are not personal expenses. Rental activities are typically reported on Schedule E and attached to your US tax return. If the home is used solely for rental purposes, then the expenses related to that home, including depreciation, are fully deductible. For a home that you use as a personal residence during part of the year and rental for part of the year, you are only allowed a deduction to the extent of the income generated.

Table 9
TRADE OR BUSINESS EXPENSES

Expenses That *Are* Deductible	Expenses That Are *Not* Deductible
Transportation expenses in the course of business, including taxi fares, automobile costs, tolls, and parking.	Commuting between one's home and one's place of business.
Travel expenses including transportation expenses and meals and lodging while away from home. The deduction for meals is limited to 50%.	Travel expenses for a spouse unless the spouse serves a bona fide business purposes.
Moving expenses.	Moving from one house to another without making a business location change that is more than 50 miles from the previous location.
Education expenses that improve your current skills.	Education expenses that train you for a new job.
Expenses for entertainment and entertainment-related meals, limited to 50%	
Taxes, including social security taxes paid by an employer, state and local income taxes, unemployment insurance taxes, real estate taxes, and foreign taxes attributable to the business.	Federal income taxes paid are not deductible in determining taxable income.
Compensation paid for reasonable salaries or other compensation for personal services.	Compensation paid to a spouse who does not perform services for the business commensurate with the compensation paid.
Business gift expenses, limited to $25 per recipient per year.	

Employee achievement awards, limited to $400 per employee, generally.	
Interest expenses.	Personal credit card and auto loan interest.
Employees' expenses, including reimbursed expenses.	The cost of regular clothing.
Home office expenses, for a portion of the home that is used exclusively, on a regular basis, as the principal place of business for your business.	An office in your home that is used by your children and other members of your family for personal use.
Contributions to employees' qualified retirement plans.	
Vacation home rental expenses.	Expenses for personal use of a vacation home.
Other business expenses.	
Expenses of professional persons including dues to professional organizations.	Expenses for membership in clubs organized for business, pleasure, recreation, or other social purposes, generally.
Landlord or tenant expenses.	Expenses incurred in connection with a land purchase contract.
Employee benefits and health insurance expenses for employees and their dependents.	Health insurance coverage for an employee's child who is older than age 27.
Life insurance premiums on an officer or employee.	

If the residence is rented for less than 15 days, then it is considered a personal residence, and you cannot deduct expenses, except for mortgage interest and real estate taxes which are allowed as itemized deductions, as with any personal residence.

If the residence is rented for more than 15 days in a year and is *not* used for personal purposes for more than the greater of 14 days or 10 percent of the total days rented, then the residence is treated as rental property. The expenses must be allocated between personal and rental days if there are any personal-use days during a year. Often, the deduction of expenses allocated to rental days can result in your expenses exceeding your income, or a rental loss. The loss may be deductible under the passive activity loss rules.

If the residence is rented for 15 days or more in a year and *is used* for personal purposes for more than the greater of 14 days or 10 percent of the total days rented, then it is treated as a personal/rental use residence. Expenses must be allocated between personal days and rental days, but expenses are allowed only to the extent of rental income. In other words, you cannot generate a passive activity loss from a personal/rental use residence.

If a residence is classified as personal/rental use, then expenses that are normally deductible as itemized deductions (e.g., real estate taxes and mortgage interest) must be allocated between personal days and rental days, based on the total days of use. If the house sat vacant for a period of time, those days cannot be used in the calculation. For example, if you rent your home for 100 days and you use your home for personal use for 120 days, then your mortgage interest and real estate taxes must be allocated 100/220 to rental expenses, and 120/220 of the expenses can be deductible as itemized deductions if you elect to itemize.

Other types of expenses that can be deducted are also allocated on the basis of total days used if the residence is classified as personal/rental use. These include operating expenses, utilities and maintenance expenses, and depreciation. It does not include any type of personal living or family expenses. It also does not include any amounts paid out for capital expenditures which are any amounts paid out for new buildings or permanent improvements or betterments made to increase the value of any property. Capital expenditures are subject to depreciation, and the depreciation is generally deductible over the life of the capital asset as determined by how the IRS classifies property. Depreciation is only allowed for a personal/rental use property to the extent that there is net income after deducting other expenses. See Table 10.

Table 10
VACATION/RENTAL HOME

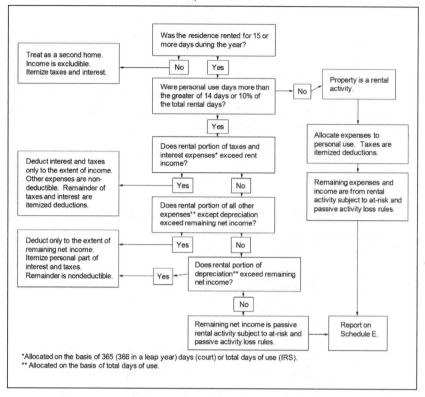

*Allocated on the basis of 365 (366 in a leap year) days (court) or total days of use (IRS).
** Allocated on the basis of total days of use.

4. Depreciation, Amortization, and Depletion Expenses

Canada uses capital cost allowance as its cost-recovery system for capital investments. In the US, we use similar systems that allow for a deduction, they are depreciation, amortization, or depletion. For purposes of understanding what is depreciated and what is amortized, tangible property is any property with physical substance, and intangible property is property that lacks substance, such as goodwill or patents. Tangible property, other than natural resources is depreciated. Intangible assets are amortized. Depletion is the method of accounting for the use of natural resources, such as oil, gas, coal, and timber. Land is not subject to any cost-recovery method.

The IRS has classified property among tangible, non-tangible, realty (real property), and personal (personal property). It further classifies property into categories based on recovery periods such as three-, five-, and ten-year property. The purpose of this discussion is not to give you all of the details of depreciation methodology; it is instead to provide you with a primer on how expenses for depreciation are available for capital assets. You should note that there are alternative depreciation methods, and if you have property that will be subject to depreciation, you should seek guidance from a tax accountant. Table 11 provides a brief list of property and classes of property subject to depreciation. Note that there are more classes of property; we are only showing the most common.

There are no capital cost-recovery deductions allowed for personal use capital assets; only for business use assets.

Table 11
CLASSES OF DEPRECIATION PROPERTY

Class of Property	Examples
3-year	Any qualified rent-to-own property
5-year	Automobiles
	Light and heavy general-purpose trucks
	Calculators, copiers, and duplicating equipment
	Any computer or peripheral equipment
	Appliances, carpets, furniture, etc. used in a rental activity
7-year	Office furniture and equipment
	Any property that does not have a class life and is not otherwise classified
15-year	Leasehold improvements placed in service before January 1, 2012
27.5 years	Residential rental property
39 years	Nonresidential real property

5. Individual Losses to Property

If you suffer damage to a personal asset or nonbusiness property, you can only deduct those losses attributable to certain events such as fire, storm, shipwreck, or other casualty or theft. These are generally known as casualty losses. The rules are that a casualty loss must result from an event that is identifiable; damaging to property; and sudden, unexpected, and unusual in nature. You can take a deduction for a casualty loss from an automobile accident only if the damage was not caused by your willful act or willful negligence. There must be damage to your property to qualify as a casualty loss.

Not all acts of God are treated as casualty losses. For example, progressive deterioration, such as erosion due to wind or water, is usually not a casualty because it does not meet the suddenness test.

Casualty losses are deducted in the year the loss occurs. No casualty loss is permitted if a reimbursement claim has a reasonable prospect of full recovery. If you have a partial claim, then only part of the claim can be deducted in the year of the casualty, and the rest is deducted when the claim is settled. If you later collect more than was expected and you are reimbursed for the amount that you deducted in a previous year, then you must report the reimbursement in gross income on the return for the year when it is received to the extent that the previous deduction resulted in a tax benefit.

The amount of the loss is calculated as the lesser of the adjusted basis of the property, or the difference between the fair market value of the property before the event and immediately after the event. Generally, an appraisal is needed to measure the loss, but the cost of repairs to the damaged property is acceptable as a method of establishing the loss in value as long as the following criteria are met:

- The repairs are necessary to restore the property to its condition immediately before the casualty.

- The amount spent for such repairs is not excessive.

- The repairs do not extend beyond the damage suffered.

- The value of the property after the repairs does not, as a result of the repairs, exceed the value of the property immediately before the casualty.

The amount of the loss for personal-use property must be reduced further by a $100 per event floor and a 10 percent of Adjusted Gross Income (AGI) aggregate floor. If the loss is spread between two taxable years, the loss in the second year is not reduced by the $100 floor but is still subject to the 10 percent of AGI floor.

Sometimes, the President of the US will declare an area as a designated disaster area, and casualties sustained in such areas can be deducted, by making an election, in the taxable year immediately preceding the taxable year in which the disaster actually occurred. This helps provide immediate relief to disaster victims in the form of accelerated tax benefits. If the disaster occurs after the previous year's tax return was filed and the taxpayer wants to make the election to claim the disaster area loss to get the accelerated tax benefit, then an amendment to the previous return should be filed.

Losses from theft are computed like other casualty losses, but the timing for recognition of the loss is different. A theft loss is deducted in the year the theft was discovered, and if there is reasonable expectation of recovering any amount from an insurance company, then no deduction is permitted. When there is a settlement, then a deduction can be taken if the recovery is less than the asset's adjusted basis. If there is a gain greater than the adjusted basis, then a gain may be recognized. If at any time a taxpayer has both a personal casualty gain and a casualty loss in the same year, the two are netted together.

6. Alimony and Child Support

Alimony payments are deductible from gross income in the year they are paid. They are a deduction for the party who pays the alimony and are reported as income for the party who receives the alimony payment.

Payments for child support are neither taxable nor deductible.

7. Contributions to Individual Retirement Accounts (IRAs)

There are several types of Individual Retirement Accounts (IRAs) available to individuals, and contributions to IRAs can be deductible or nondeductible. If you made contributions to a traditional IRA, you may be able to take an IRA deduction. However, you must have taxable compensation effectively connected with a US trade or business to do so.

There are complicated rules for IRAs and qualified retirement plans, and we do not intend to explain the complications in any detail.

In a very general sense, there are traditional IRAs and Roth IRAs. To be eligible to make a contribution to an IRA, you must have earned income in the US, which includes alimony and wage payments from a US taxpayer employer. Generally, amounts held and earned in traditional IRAs are not taxed until a distribution is made, so when a contribution is made to a traditional IRA, a deduction is allowed. Amounts contributed to Roth IRAs are not deductible, and the amounts, including earnings and profits that are accumulated in a Roth IRA, are usually tax free when they are withdrawn. In very simple terms, traditional IRAs are generally tax free when contributed and are taxed when distributions are paid out, and contributions to Roth IRAs are taxed when contributed and distributions are tax free. There are limitations on when distributions can be made.

In 2012, the maximum annual combined contribution that can be made to all of an individual's IRAs is $5,000. If an individual is age 50 or older, he or she can contribute an additional catch-up contribution of $1,000 per year. The person has until the due date of his or her return to make contributions. This means that he or she has until April 15 of the year following the tax year to make a contribution to his or her IRA.

If either you are or your spouse is active participant in an employer-sponsored qualified retirement plan such as a 401(k) or a 403(b), then the amount of your deduction for a contribution to an IRA can be limited. When a single person or a head of household is an active participant in an employer's retirement plan, the IRA deduction begins to phase out when the taxpayer's AGI reaches $58,000 and completely phases out when AGI reaches $68,000 (in 2012). For married individuals who file a joint return, the phase out range is $92,000 to $112,000.

You can only make contributions to a traditional IRA if you are younger than age 70.5, and upon reaching age 70.5, you will be required to make minimum required distributions annually from a traditional IRA.

It is very easy to create an IRA account with a bank or custodian. Before you do so, however, you should seek advice from a tax accountant or retirement plan specialist if you are interested in contributing to an IRA. There can be penalties for contributing funds to an IRA that are in excess of what you are permitted.

8. Moving Expenses

Employees or self-employed persons can deduct reasonable expenses for moving themselves and their families if the move is a result of a work-related relocation. For the expenses to be deductible, a distance test and a length-of-employment test must be met.

The new principal place of work must be at least 50 miles farther from your former home than the old job location was. If you have no former job location, the new job location must be at least 50 miles from your former home. You cannot deduct the moving expense when you are returning to your home in Canada or moving to a foreign job site, these expenses would have to be deducted in the foreign country, if allowed. The rules are specific to eliminate a moving deduction for taxpayers who purchase a new home in the same general area without changing their place of employment.

To meet the length-of-employment test, an employee must be employed on a full-time basis at the new location for 39 weeks in the 12-month period following the move. If the taxpayer is self-employed, he or she must work in the new location for 78 weeks during the next two years.

If you deduct moving expenses to the US, you cannot deduct travel expenses. Moving expenses result from a change in your principal place of business, and travel expenses are based on a temporary absence from your principal place of business. You can only deduct moving expenses that are not reimbursed or paid by your employer.

9. Health Savings Accounts (HSA)

For US resident taxpayers who have US health coverage, there are several types of medical savings accounts that typically link a high deductible health plan with a tax favored account, such as a health savings account (HSA), an Archer medical savings account (MSA) or a health reimbursement arrangement (HRA). These accounts are tax favored because the contributions to these accounts can be tax deductible, and distributions to pay qualified medical expenses are not taxable.

An HSA can be created if an individual has a high deductible health plan, is not covered by another other medical plan that is not a high deductible plan, is not enrolled in Medicare, and is not claimed as a dependent on somebody else's tax return. If you meet these requirements in 2012, you can make tax-deductible contributions of up to $3,100 if you are covered under a self-coverage plan or $6,250 if you are covered under a family coverage plan. Different limits apply for MSAs. If you make contributions in excess of these limits, there is a 6 percent excise tax in addition to the deductions being nondeductible. If you are older than age 55, you can increase your annual contribution by an additional $1,000 per year.

A high deductible health plan is a plan that has a minimum annual deductible of $1,200 per year for self-coverage plans and $2,400 for family coverage plans for 2012. There are limits on how much your out-of-pocket expenses can be for these plans. For example, the annual out-of-pocket expenses for a self-coverage plan cannot exceed $6,050 ($12,100 per family) in 2012.

Qualified medical expenses include medical, dental, and vision care, as well as prescription drugs and premiums for long-term care. Generally, premiums for insurance are not qualified medical expenses unless they are for insurance coverage during periods of unemployment.

10. Qualified Education Expenses and Student Loan Interest

There are several deductions available for taxpayers who have qualified education expenses. Through 2011, taxpayers can deduct interest paid on any qualified education loan. The debt must be held by the taxpayer and must have been used solely to pay for qualified higher education expenses. This deduction is above the line for Adjusted Gross Income (AGI) and is limited to a maximum deduction of $2,500. It is phased out when a single taxpayer's AGI is between $50,000 and $75,000 (double that for joint taxpayers).

Deductions can be taken above the line for AGI for tuition and related expenses paid for enrollment or attendance at an accredited postsecondary institution for his or her own expenses or a spouse's or dependent's expenses. The maximum allowed deduction, through 2011, is $4,000, and is phased out for single taxpayers with AGI between $65,000 and $80,000 (double for joint taxpayers).

Education expenses that improve skills required in your present job or meet the express requirements of your employer may be deductible below the line from AGI as education expenses. Generally, these expenses are allowed as business expenses for the employer, even if you are self-employed. If you are self-employed, you will want to report the expenses as business expenses. If your employer does not pay for these expenses and you are not self-employed, then you can generally deduct the unreimbursed education expenditures related to your job as itemized deductions, subject to 2 percent of AGI.

11. Exemptions

The US tax system uses exemptions in part based on an idea that a taxpayer with a small amount of income should be exempt from taxation. Exemptions free a specified amount of income from tax ($3,800 for 2012). The Internal Revenue Code allows a personal exemption for the taxpayer and for the spouse if a joint return is filed. Dependency exemptions can also be claimed for dependents who meet certain tests.

A resident alien can claim a personal exemption deduction from Adjusted Gross Income (AGI) on his or her tax return. In addition, if he or she has any dependents, then an additional exemption can be claimed for each dependent. For resident alien taxpayers who are filing a joint return with their spouse, exemptions can be claimed for both spouses.

Note: Dependents and spouses MUST have either an ITIN or SSN in order to be claimed as dependents.

Nonresident aliens engaged in a trade or business in the US can only claim one personal exemption. For Canadians, you can also claim a personal exemption for your spouse if your spouse had no gross income for US tax purposes and is not claimed on another US taxpayer's return. You can also claim exemptions for your dependents.

There are several rules for determining who qualifies as a dependent. In its most simplest sense, a qualifying child dependent is generally a child younger than age 19, or younger than age 24 if he or she is a full-time student, who has lived with you for more than one half of the year, except if he or she is away for school, and who has not provided for more than one-half of his or her own support for the year. Certain qualifying relatives can also be claimed as dependents including siblings, parents, grandparents, aunts, or uncles. These individuals must meet minimum income requirements and support tests in order to be claimed as dependents.

The exemption amount is adjusted annually for inflation. For 2012, the exemption is $3,800 per exemption. The exemption amount is reduced for taxpayers whose AGI exceeds a threshold amount.

12. Standard Deductions or Itemized Deductions

Generally, a taxpayer has the choice of taking a standard deduction, which is an amount determined each year by Congress, or itemized deductions, which are several expenses that can be "itemized" on Schedule A. Taxpayers whose total aggregate itemized deductions are less than the standard deduction can choose to take a standard deduction amount instead of the itemized deduction. Either itemized deductions or the standard deductions are subtracted from a taxpayer's Adjusted Gross Income (AGI) to determine taxable income.

12.1 Standard deductions

The standard deduction is made of up two components, a "basic standard deduction" as shown in Table 12 and an "additional standard deduction" as shown in Table 13. Only taxpayers who are age 65 or older or blind qualify for the additional standard deduction.

Table 12
STANDARD DEDUCTION AMOUNTS

Filing Status	Standard Deduction Amounts	
	2011	2012
Single	$5,800	$5,950
Married, Filing Jointly	$11,600	$11,900
Head of Household	$8,500	$8,700
Married, Filing Separately	$5,800	$5,950

Table 13
ADDITIONAL DEDUCTION AMOUNTS

Filing Status	Standard Deduction Amounts	
	2011	2012
Single	$1,450	$1,450
Married, Filing Jointly	$2,300	$2,300
Head of Household	$1,450	$1,450
Married, Filing Separately	$1,150	$1,150

For a taxpayer who is both blind and older than age 65, he or she can claim two additional deduction amounts, and if a couple is both older than age 65 and are both blind, they can claim four additional deduction amounts of $1,150 each.

Nonresident aliens are not eligible for the standard deduction. Dual-status taxpayers (taxpayers who change status between nonresident and resident during the year) also cannot use a standard deduction. Nonresident aliens and dual-status taxpayers can, however, report certain itemized deductions. You should also note that nonresident aliens and dual-status taxpayers cannot file using either a head of household or a married filing jointly status.

12.2 Itemized deductions

Generally, personal expenses are disallowed; however, Congress has allowed certain personal expenses to be deductible as itemized deductions. These include medical expenses, certain taxes, mortgage interest, investment interest, and charitable contributions. Itemized deductions include, but are not limited to the following:

- Medical expenses in excess of 7.5 percent of Adjusted Gross Income (AGI)

- State and local income taxes

- Real estate taxes

- Personal property taxes

- Interest on home mortgage

- Investment interest, subject to a limit

- Charitable contributions, subject to limits

- Casualty and theft losses in excess of 10 percent of AGI, plus $100

- Miscellaneous expenses such as the following, to the extent they exceed 2 percent of AGI:

  - Union dues

  - Professional dues and subscriptions

  - Certain educational expenses

- Tax return preparation fees

- Investment counsel fees

- Unreimbursed employee business expenses, subject to limits.

Resident aliens can claim the same itemized deductions as US citizens using Schedule A of Form 1040. Nonresident aliens can deduct certain itemized deductions if you receive income effectively connected with a US trade or business. The deductions available to nonresident aliens include state and local income taxes, charitable contributions to US organizations, casualty and theft losses, and miscellaneous deductions. Nonresident aliens can claim itemized deductions on Schedule A of Form 1040NR.

13. State and Local Taxes

State, local, and foreign taxes paid on real property are deductible. Taxes on personal property are generally not deductible unless they are assessed in relation to the value of the property. Special assessments are also not deductible. Instead, any payments for special assessments such as sidewalks, sewers, or streets are added to the adjusted basis of the property.

State and local income taxes are deductible as itemized deductions. If you overpay state income taxes and receive a refund in a year following the year the deduction was taken, then the refund is included in your gross income for Adjusted Gross Income (AGI) in the year the refund was received.

14. Interest Expenses

Personal (consumer) interest is not deductible. This includes credit card interest, interest on vehicle loans, other interest that is not investment interest, home mortgage interest, or business interest.

When a resident taxpayer borrows money to acquire investments, the interest paid on the borrowed funds is deductible, but is limited to the net investment income for the year. Investment income is gross income from interest, dividends, annuities, and royalties not derived in the ordinary course of a trade or business, and not from a passive activity such as real estate. This does not include capital gains as investment income, unless an election is made. However, if the election is made, it can result in your capital gains being taxed at higher ordinary tax rates instead of capital gains rates. Interest on debt incurred to purchase or carry tax exempt securities is not deductible.

If you do not have enough investment income during a year to fully deduct all of the investment interest paid, then you can carry it over to future years, without a limit on the length of the carryover period.

If the interest is related to rental or royalty property, then the deduction is allowed as a deduction from rental income on Schedule E — above the line for Adjusted Gross Income (AGI). Interest on debt in relation to a business is allowed as an expense of the business on Schedule C — above the line for AGI. Otherwise, all investment interest that is not related to rental, business, or royalty property is an itemized deduction on Schedule A.

Qualified residence interest for US resident taxpayers can be deductible. This is interest paid or accrued during the taxable year on an indebtedness that is secured by any property that is a qualified residence of the taxpayer. Qualified residence interest is either interest on acquisition indebtedness or interest on home equity loans.

There are limits to the amount of qualified residence interest that can be deducted. A qualified residence includes the taxpayer's principal residence and one other residence of the taxpayer or spouse. If a taxpayer has more than one second residence, he or she can make the selection each year of which one is the second qualified residence. A residence is a house, cooperative apartment, condominium, mobile home, or boat or motor home that has living quarters, which is described as having sleeping accommodations and toilet and cooking facilities. The interest deduction is also limited to interest paid on aggregate qualified residence indebtedness of $1,000,000 (or $500,000 for a married individual filing a separate return) plus $100,000 of home equity indebtedness (or $50,000 for a married individual filing a separate return).

Points paid to purchase or improve a home can be deducted as interest in the year the points are paid. Points paid to refinance an existing home cannot be immediately expensed but must be capitalized and amortized as interest expense over the life of the new loan, unless the proceeds are used for improvements. If the points are paid by the seller, they are not deductible by the buyer.

Prepayment penalties resulting from paying off a loan in full or in a lump-sum before its term can be deductible as qualified mortgage interest expense, as long as the general rules for deductibility of interest are followed.

A taxpayer cannot deduct any interest paid on behalf of another individual. Interest is generally deductible in the year it is paid.

15. Medical Expenses

Medical expenses are deductible for the care of the taxpayer, his or her spouse, and dependents, as long as the medical expenses have not been reimbursed. However, the medical expense deduction is limited to the amount that those expenses exceed 7.5 percent of the taxpayer's Adjusted Gross Income (AGI). This threshold will increase to 10 percent of AGI for tax years beginning after December 31, 2012, except for taxpayers and their spouses who are age 65 or older before the close of the tax year, in which case the 7.5 percent of AGI threshold will continue to apply for tax years 2013 through 2016.

Deductible medical expenses include expenditures for the "diagnosis, cure, mitigation, treatment, or prevention of disease, or for the purpose of affecting any structure of function of the body."

The following is a partial list of deductible medical items:

- Medical care including dental, mental, and hospital

- Prescription drugs

- Special equipment such as wheelchairs, crutches, artificial limbs, eyeglasses (including contact lenses), hearing aids

- Transportation for medical care

- Medical and hospital insurance premiums

- Cost of alcohol and drug rehabilitation

The following is a partial list of nondeductible medical items:

- Funeral, burial, or cremation services

- Nonprescription drugs (except insulin)

- Bottled water

- Toiletries or cosmetics

- Diaper service, maternity clothes

- Programs for the general improvement of health including weight reduction, health spas, stop-smoking clinics, and social activities such as dancing or swimming lessons

- Unnecessary cosmetic surgery

Amounts paid for cosmetic surgery can only be deducted if deemed necessary. It is necessary when it corrects a deformity arising from a congenital abnormality, a personal injury, or a disfiguring disease.

The cost of care in a nursing home or home for the aged, including meals and lodging, can be included in deductible medical expenses if the primary reason for being in the home is medical care. If the primary reason for being there is personal, costs for medical or nursing care can be included, but the costs of meals and lodging must be excluded.

Tuition expenses of a dependent at a special school may be deductible as a medical expense. The deduction for the costs of the special school is allowed if a principal reason for sending the individual to the school is because of a special education system for physically or medically handicapped persons. The costs of lodging and meals resulting from going to the special school may also be deductible as medical expenses.

Some capital improvements can qualify as medical expenses, such as the cost of home-related capital expenditures incurred to enable a physically handicapped person to live independently and productively in the home. This could include ramps, widening hallways and doorways, installing support bars, and adjusting electrical outlets and fixtures. Typically, improvements increase the cost basis of the home, but when the expenses are used as medical expense deductions, there is no increase in the cost basis of the home.

The costs for transportation, meals, and lodging for medical treatment can also be deductible as medical expenses. These include bus, taxi, train, air fare, ambulance services, and out-of-pocket expenses for the use of an automobile. An allowance of 23 cents per mile can be used instead of actual out-of-pocket automobile expenses. This is the rate in effect as of January 1, 2012. This allowance includes the transportation expenses of a parent who must accompany a child who is receiving medical care or a nurse or other person giving assistance to someone who is traveling to get medical care and cannot travel alone. The deduction for lodging while away from home can be taken only when the lodging is primarily for and essential for the medical care. The deduction cannot exceed $50 per night for the patient and another $50 if a person must travel with the patient. Meals for persons who are not the patient are generally not deductible.

Medical insurance premiums, paid by you, can also be deducted as medical expenses. This is only if the costs are paid by you and are not reimbursed or paid for by any other person, entity, or your employer. Long-term care insurance premiums can also be deductible, but there are dollar limits on the amount that can be deductible; those limits are shown in Table 14.

Table 14
LIMITS ON MEDICAL DEDUCTIONS

(This table lists the limits of the long-term care premiums that can be deducted as medical deductions)

Taxpayers Age at End of Tax Year	2012 Limit
40 and younger	$350
Older than 40 but not older than 50	$660
Older than 50 but not older than 60	$1,310
Older than 60 but not older than 70	$3,500
Older than 70	$4,370

Medical expenses must be deducted in the year the expenses were paid, except for when a taxpayer dies. If the medical expenses of a deceased person are paid within one year following the date of death, they can be treated as being paid at the time they were incurred. This means that these expenses may be reported on the final income tax return of the decedent or on earlier returns if the expenses were incurred before the year of death.

16. Employee Educational Expenses

If education expenses for US resident taxpayers are incurred in the pursuit of maintaining or improving skills required in a taxpayer's employment or other trade or business, even if they lead to a degree, then they may be deductible as non-reimbursed employee expenses.

They cannot be deductible if they are not required to meet minimum education requirements for a taxpayer's current job or to qualify the taxpayer for a new trade or business. If the expenses are paid for or are reimbursed by an employer, then they cannot be deducted by the employee.

17. Charitable Contributions

Generally, any contributions made to qualified US charitable organizations can be deductible as itemized deductions in the year the payment is made, subject to several qualifiers and limitations. A charitable contribution must have a donative intent with the absence of consideration. The transfer must be made with the motive of disinterested generosity.

Contributions of services are not deductible. However, unreimbursed expenses involved for providing your contribution of services, including out-of-pocket transportation costs, may be deductible. In lieu of out-of-pocket transportation costs in 2012, a standard mileage rate of 14 cents per mile can be deducted, plus parking fees and tolls. Deductions for reasonable costs of lodging and meals can be deductible for time spent away from home for performing donated services.

Nondeductible items include dues to clubs, lodges, costs of bingo or lottery tickets, costs of tuition, the value of your blood given to a blood bank, donations to homeowners' associations, gifts to individuals, and rental values of property used by a charity. Qualified organizations include states or possessions of the US, organizations situated in the US organized and operated for religious, charitable, scientific, literary, or education purposes, or for the prevention of cruelty to children or animals, veterans' organizations, fraternal organizations, or cemetery companies. Contributions to foreign organizations are not deductible; however, you may be able to deduct contributions to US charitable organizations that transfer funds for foreign charitable needs. The IRS publishes a list of organizations that have applied for and received tax exempt status as charitable organizations.

If your total charitable contributions are less than $250 in any year, you do not need to include written substantiation of the contributions. However, if the deductions are greater than $250, you will need to specify the amount of cash and a description of any property other than cash contributed. You must have a written statement from the charitable organization confirming the contribution.

For noncash contributions of property, you should refer to Publication 526 for details on what you will need for substantiation of the contribution. If the value of the contribution is more than $500, then you will have to complete and attach the Noncash Charitable Contributions (Form 8283) to your return. If the value of the donated property is $5,000 or more, you will have to get a qualified appraisal. Taxpayers who donate a vehicle, truck, boat, or aircraft valued at more than $500 must obtain a Contributions of Motor Vehicles, Boats, and Airplanes (Form 1098-C) from the charity, and if the charity sells the property, then the deduction may be limited to the proceeds that the charity was able to receive from the sale.

If ordinary income property is donated, the deduction is equal to the fair market value of the property less the amount of ordinary income that would have been reported if the property was sold. Ordinary income property is any property that, if sold, would result in the recognition of ordinary income. This can be inventory in the taxpayer's trade or business, a work of art created by the donor, or a manuscript prepared by the donor, or short-term capital gain property. In most instances, the charitable deduction for ordinary income property is limited to the adjusted basis of the property.

The contribution of long-term capital gain property generally results in a deduction equal to the fair market value of the property at the time of contribution. Special rules apply if property is contributed to a private foundation. There are also special rules for tangible personal property, which is property that is neither realty, nor intangible property such as stock or securities. If tangible property is contributed to a public charity, such as a museum, church, or university, the charitable deduction may have to be reduced if the property is put to a use that is unrelated to its purpose. For example, if you donate a piece of artwork to a museum, and it is not kept by the museum but is instead immediately sold at a fund-raising auction, it was not used for its intended purpose as a piece of artwork. If the art is retained in the museum's collection, then it would be considered to be used for its intended use and would be fully deductible.

Each taxpayer has limits on the amounts that can be deductible in any year for charitable contributions. Contributions made to public charities cannot be deducted if they exceed 50 percent of an individual's Adjusted Gross Income (AGI) for the year. A 30 percent ceiling applies for contributions made to private nonoperating foundations, except for long-term capital gain property contributed to private nonoperating foundations, in which case it is subject to a 20 percent of AGI ceiling. All excess contributions can be carried over for five years.

Note: The Treaty allows for a charitable deduction to Canadian Charities as long as the contribution meets two criteria:

- The charity would have met the tax exempt criteria if it were in the US.

- You must have income from Canada that equals or exceeds the deduction claimed.

Because this deduction is permitted under the Treaty, you must file Treaty-Based Return Position Disclosure under Section 6114 or 7701(b) (Form 8833) for the deduction to be valid.

18. Miscellaneous Itemized Deductions

The following expenses are a partial list of items that can be deducted as miscellaneous itemized deductions:

- Gambling losses up to the amount of gambling winnings.

- Impairment-related work expenses of a handicapped person.

- Federal estate tax on income in respect of a decedent.

- An unrecovered investment in an annuity contract when an annuity ceases as a result of death.

The following is a partial list of items that can be deducted if, in total, they exceed 2 percent of the taxpayer's Adjusted Gross Income (AGI):

- Professional dues to membership organizations.

- Uniforms or other clothing that cannot be used for normal wear.

- Fees for preparing tax returns or fees for tax litigation before the IRS or the courts.

- Job hunting costs.

- Fees paid for a safe deposit box used to store papers and documents relating to taxable income-producing investments.

- Investment management expenses for the management of taxable US investments.

- Appraisal fees to determine the fair market value of the property involved in a casualty loss or a donation.

- Hobby losses up to the amount of hobby income.

- Unreimbursed employee expenses.

You may be able to deduct ordinary and necessary travel expenses while you are working in the US if you are on a temporary assignment that is realistically expected to, and does last for one year or less. These expenses would be miscellaneous itemized deductions subject to 2 percent of your AGI. If you qualify, you may be able to deduct expenses for your transportation, lodging, and 50 percent of the cost of your meals. If you are reimbursed by your employer for these expenses, or if your employer pays these costs, then you would not be able to deduct the expenses. You would be able to deduct your expenses only and not the expenses for anyone else, including members of your family.

Note that most, if not all of the itemized deductions reported on Schedule A are for personal expenses only and not for expenses related to the production of income, in connection with a trade or business, unless they are unreimbursed expenses that you paid out of your own pocket. If the expense is incurred as a result of a passive or rental activity, it is generally a deduction for AGI and reported on Schedule E, and if the expense is incurred in connection with a trade or business, it is a deduction for AGI and is reported on Schedule C. Also, expenses that are reimbursed or paid by an employer are not deductible by the employee.

19. Credits

Congress has often used tax credits to achieve social or economic objectives to promote equity among different types of taxpayers. Tax credits should not be confused with income tax deductions. Tax credits are not affected by the tax rate of the taxpayer; they are a direct reduction of the tax.

Certain credits are refundable, meaning that if the amount of the credit exceeds the taxpayer's tax liability, the excess is paid to the taxpayer. However, nonrefundable credits are not paid if they exceed the taxpayer's tax liability.

Some nonrefundable credits, such as the foreign tax credit, are subject to carryover provisions if they exceed an allowable amount during the year. The foreign tax credit is not discussed here because a full chapter is dedicated to it (see Chapter 5).

Like every other aspect of the US Federal income tax system, the rules can be complicated. If you want to use any of the credits available to you, you should seek advice from a qualified tax accountant. We are merely introducing you to the concepts.

19.1 Child and dependent credit

A nonrefundable credit may be available to taxpayers who incur employment-related expenses for child or dependent care, for children under age 13. The credit is based on a percentage of actual dependent care expenses that were incurred so that the taxpayer could work.

The maximum credit $1,050 for one qualifying dependent or $2,100 if two or more qualifying dependents are involved is available, and is available for taxpayers with Adjusted Gross Income (AGI) of less than $15,000. The credit starts to get reduced when AGI exceeds $15,000 and is capped when AGI reaches $43,000. For taxpayers with AGI of greater than $43,000, they can claim the minimum credit of $600 for one dependent or $1,200 for two or more dependents. Married taxpayers must generally file a joint return to claim this credit, and because the credit is per dependent, there is no additional allowance for a couple filing jointly.

19.2 Credit for the elderly or disabled

A nonrefundable credit is available to taxpayers who are 65 years old or are permanently disabled. This credit is 15 percent of an initial amount which is $5,000 for single individuals and $7,500 for married couples filing jointly. For married couples filing separately, the amount is $3,750. The amount is reduced by amounts received as pension, annuity, or disability benefits that are excludable from gross income, and then reduced by one-half of the taxpayer's AGI in excess of $7,500 for single taxpayers or $5,000 per each married taxpayer.

The eligibility requirements and the tax computation for this credit are complicated. An individual may elect to have the IRS compute his or her tax and the amount of tax credit.

19.3 Child tax credit

A credit is available for taxpayers who have one or more qualifying children that they also claim as dependents. This is separate from the child and dependent care credit. The credit is $1,000 per child through 2012, and decreases to $500 per child beginning in 2013. The credit is phased out when modified Adjusted Gross Income (AGI) reaches $110,000 for joint taxpayers and $75,000 for single taxpayers. The credit is reduced by $50 for every $1,000 of modified AGI in excess of those thresholds. The credit can be partially refundable.

19.4 Earned income credit

This credit is a refundable credit that is available to low-income individuals who have an Adjusted Gross Income (AGI) below a certain level, have a valid Social Security number, and use a filing status other than married filing separately. You must be a US citizen or resident alien and have no foreign income to be eligible for this credit.

The determination of the amount of the credit and the phase-out limits for this credit depend on how many dependent children you have. The credit is based on earned income, and the maximum credit for taxpayers with one qualifying child, for example, is $3,169 in 2012. A maximum credit in 2012 for three or more children is $5,891. If you have no qualifying dependent children, your maximum credit is $475.

19.5 Education credits

There are credits available to help qualifying low- and middle-income individuals defray the costs of higher education. These credits are generally nonrefundable and are available for qualifying tuition and related expenses incurred by students seeking college, graduate degrees, or vocational training. These credits are not available for nonresident alien taxpayers.

The American Opportunity Credit is a credit for 100 percent of the first $2,000 of qualified tuition and related expenses plus 25 percent of the next $2,000, for a total maximum credit of $2,500 per eligible student per year. Forty percent of the credit is refundable, which means that you may be able to receive up to $1,000, even if you owe no taxes. The credit phases out for taxpayers with modified Adjusted Gross Income (AGI) between $80,000 and $90,000 (double for married taxpayers who file joint returns). The credit cannot be taken by married taxpayers who file separate returns. This credit is available for tax years 2009 through 2013. This credit replaced a Hope Scholarship Credit which was available in previous years.

A Lifetime Learning Credit is available for qualified tuition expenses paid on the first $10,000 of tuition. It is a one-time credit and is limited to $2,000. The credit is phased out for single taxpayers when modified AGI reaches $52,000 in 2012 and completely phases out when modified AGI exceeds $62,000 in 2012. For joint taxpayers, the phase out is $104,000 and $124,000 in 2012.

19.6 Retirement savings contributions credit

In cases of low-income taxpayers, a nonrefundable credit is available for taxpayers who make a contribution to a qualified retirement savings plan. This includes contributions made to a traditional or Roth IRA, elective deferrals to a 401(k) plan or 403(b) plan, or other qualified plan. The credit is available for taxpayers whose 2012 Adjusted Gross Income (AGI) is less than $57,500 for joint returns, $43,125 for heads of household, and $28,750 for single filers. The maximum credit amount is $1,000 and is calculated as a percentage multiplied by the contributions, up to $2,000 per year, to qualified retirement plans during the year. This credit is available to residents and nonresident aliens.

19.7 Other credits

In addition to the credits that we discussed above, there are several credits available for very specific circumstances. (Foreign tax credits are discussed in Chapter 5.) The following is a partial list of other credits that may be available:

- A first-time home-buyer credit was available for qualified homeowners who purchased a home before May 1, 2010, to be their principal residence. This type of credit has been available, in different forms, many times and may be reintroduced at some point. This credit would not be available to nonresident aliens.

- A refundable adoption credit for qualified adoption expenses. In 2012, the credit reverts back to being nonrefundable.

- Health insurance premium assistance refundable credit for very low-income individuals and families. This credit will begin for tax years ending after December 31, 2013, and is meant to help with the cost of federally mandated insurance costs for very low-income persons. This credit will be available for lawful resident aliens who are not eligible for Medicaid; however, the credit is for households whose income is below the federal poverty level.

- There are nonrefundable credits available for energy efficient nonbusiness property and improvements, such as residential doors and windows, insulation, heat pumps, furnaces, air conditioners, and hot water heaters. The credit is available for qualified energy efficiency improvements installed between January 2008 and January 1, 2012.

- There are nonrefundable credits available for alternative motor vehicles. Various vehicles qualify for credits, and the credits are different for each type of vehicle. The credits have been available for plug-in electric drive motor vehicles, hybrid vehicles, alternative fuel vehicles, and alternative fuel refueling property.

- Businesses have several credits available, including the alternative motor vehicles credits and energy efficient property credits. There is an extensive list of credits available for special situations. For example, a commonly used business credit is a work opportunity credit, which is available to businesses for hiring hard-to-employ individuals.

9

Tax Planning

The items discussed in this chapter are more prone to change than most other parts of the tax code. Be sure to consult with a tax advisor before implementing any of the tax-planning strategies mentioned here or elsewhere.

Unlike Canada, the US has numerous tax-planning opportunities. You may have heard Warren Buffet, one of the richest men in the world, say that his tax rate is lower than his secretary's. Because Mr. Buffet is able to structure his income in such a way as to receive mostly long-term capital gains (taxed at a flat 15 percent tax rate), qualified dividends (taxed at a flat 15 percent), and municipal bond interest (tax free), his effective tax rate was approximately 15 percent, while he claimed his secretary, whose only source of income was wages, was in the 25 percent tax bracket. Without getting into the social, economic, or moral discussion on whether this treatment is right or wrong, we want to discuss various tax opportunities available in the US.

While it is common for Canadians to use Canadian-Controlled Private Corporations to defer taxes, it is rare for Americans to use regular corporations (we call them C Corporations). There are a number of reasons for this, but the tax reasons are the following:

- C Corporations are subject to double tax. Whereas in Canada, the individual receives a dividend credit to offset the tax previously paid by the corporation, the US has no such credit and therefore both the corporation and the individual pay tax on the same income, creating double tax.

- Capital gains within a corporation do not receive the lower tax rate; the income is taxed at the marginal tax rate.

While these concerns are less of a problem for service businesses where there are few assets, little or no chance for a capital gain, and bonuses can be paid out to assure there will be no corporate tax, the non-tax benefits of other forms of ownership such as a Limited Liability Company (LLC), make the LLC the entity of choice for most business owners.

Also, unlike Canada, US tax law allows for a number of tax-deferred, tax-free, and tax-favored opportunities, in addition to retirement savings plans. The rest of this chapter will discuss various tax-planning opportunities available to US taxpayers.

Before we start, let's clarify a point of confusion. There are a number of stories claiming that Canada is a more tax-friendly place to live than the US, (Friendlier, we will give you that — tax friendlier, no way!) Those making this claim, make two true statements:

1. The US and Canada have very similar income tax rates, and in some cases, lower tax rates than the US.

2. Canadian corporate tax rates are lower than the US corporate tax rates, then jump to the conclusion that Canada must be a more tax-friendly place to live.

We prepare US and Canadian tax returns day after day, year after year, and we can see that in nearly every case the Canadian tax is higher than the US tax.

The corporate tax rate is the easiest point to discuss, so we will discuss it first. Yes, Canadian corporate tax rates are lower; in fact, the US is among the world's highest corporate tax rates. However, as we explained above, almost no one uses corporations in the US, and the ones that do, generally pay little or no corporate tax. There is one big exception to this and that is public companies like the ones listed on a stock exchange. However, the people that run those companies are small in number and are not the readers of this book. So for those of you reading this book, the corporate tax rate could be 100 percent and it would not make any difference because you will not be using a US corporation anyway.

The personal income tax rates are also easy to explain. The reason the tax rates are similar, yet Americans pay lower overall personal taxes is, in large part, due to the fact that there are so many tax-planning opportunities. In Canada, there is relatively little difference between your gross income and your taxable income. Whereas in the US, there can not only be substantial differences between gross income and taxable income, the income that is reported may be subject to special, lower, tax rates. In addition, some of the income can be deferred to later years or be completely tax-free; you can even choose to live in a state that has no state income tax. Add to those facts, that while the marginal tax rates are similar, the income at which you reach those tax rates are substantially different. For example, in 2011, you were not in the highest US federal tax bracket of 35 percent until you had taxable income of more than $379,150. Compare that to Canada where you are paying the maximum tax rate starting at $128,800 of income. Based on our experience, you can expect to pay about one-third less as a US taxpayer. Of course, this could be more or less depending on where in Canada you live, where in the US you choose to live, and the type of income you are earning.

Note: We believe that the US is Canada's best tax haven. For more information of why we believe this is so, you can read the book by Robert Keats, titled, *A Canadian's Best Tax Haven: The US*. Here is the link if you wish to order the book: www.self-counsel.com/default/personal-finance.html. (The book is also available in electronic format.)

1. Tax Planning in General

When thinking about tax planning, it is good to start with the big picture before getting into the details. Tax planning falls into the following eight general categories:

- Convert taxable income into tax-free income (municipal bond interest)

- Convert taxable income into tax-preferred income (long-term capital gains and qualified dividends)

- Defer income into future years (retirement plans, installment sales, tax-free exchanges, annuities, US savings bonds)

- Take advantage of special tax breaks (education)

- Take advantage of special tax credits (energy, child care, adoption)

- Income splitting (with spouse or children)

- Convert normally nondeductible expense into deductible expenses (business and rental expenses)

- Timing (accelerating or deferring income or expenses to maximize your tax brackets)

Many of these items are discussed in detail in Chapter 7, but we want to pull the idea of tax planning into a coherent concept in this chapter rather than leaving it to you to gather the bits and pieces throughout the book.

Note: When thinking about tax planning, you must consider the outcome over at least two years. The easiest example to show this is, if you choose to defer income and accelerate expenses in 2012 that means that 2013 will have to include the income you deferred and will not have the expenses you took in 2012. Some cases where this might make sense are if you had an exceptionally good year in your business and you do not expect that level of income again next year. Alternatively, you could be retiring in 2013 and expect your income to drop significantly.

2. Specific Tax-Planning Opportunities

The following sections discuss specific tax-planning opportunities such as using your principal residence, other real estate investments, securities, and EE and I bonds.

2.1 Your principal residence

One tax break that is better in Canada than in the US is the exclusion of capital gains on your principal residence. As you know, Canada allows an unlimited exclusion, with certain limitations based on the size of the lot. The US allows an exemption of $250,000 per person. This exclusion applies if the residence was your principal residence for at least two of the last five years. A home, condo, mobile home, boat, RV, etc. can qualify as a principal residence as long as it has sleeping, eating, and toileting accommodations. If you have multiple homes, the rules for determining your principal residence are similar to those in Canada; basically it means where you spend most of your time.

If you rented your home, you will have to pro-rate the exclusion, even if you meet the two- out of five-year rule. This most frequently happens when you do not sell your home in Canada prior to moving to the US. Rather than leave the home vacant, you decide to rent your Canadian home until you sell it. Even if you sell the home within three years so that you meet the two- out of five-year test, you will not be able to exclude the entire $250,000 per person.

2.2 Other real estate investments

US tax law provides many incentives for real estate investment. While many of the tax incentives are similar to Canada, some are not. Some incentives that are similar are the ability to accelerate expenses through depreciation (capital cost allowance) and preferable tax treatment on the sale. One big difference that the US provides is the ability to rollover your profits into a new property in what is called a tax-free exchange.

Note: There are "passive activity" and "passive loss" rules that make real estate investing complicated, from a tax perspective.

2.3 Securities

One of the legitimate knocks on the US tax law is that it is too complex. Securities and real estate law are examples of this. Just as in the real estate sections above, we will only talk in generalities.

Common stocks allow you to defer gain and generally pay a flat 15 percent capital gains tax if the stock was held for more than one year. Gains held a year or less are subject to ordinary income tax rates. Dividends also are taxed at a preferred rate of 15 percent. Both of these laws are expected to change in 2013.

Municipal bonds are state and local government obligations. The interest paid on these obligations is free from federal tax and free from state income tax of the state they were issued. Of course, it is not quite that simple. When considering the purchase, you have to consider whether the bond is for public purpose, qualified private activity, or non-qualifying private activity. Non-qualifying private activity bonds are taxable at the federal level and tax free at the state level. Qualified private activity bonds are tax free, but have alternative minimum tax implications.

2.4 Series EE bonds and I bonds

These bonds are issued by the US government and have a fixed rate of interest and are guaranteed by the full faith and credit of the US I bonds, or inflation adjusted bonds provide a return that rises and falls with inflation. The bond has a minimum guaranteed rate and that rate can be supplemented if inflation increases. Both bonds can be bought for as little as $25, with a limit of $10,000 per year. Bonds must be held at least 12 months before they can be redeemed. If redeemed before five years, three months of interest is lost. Interest on these bonds is deferred until redeemed, or 30 years, whichever comes first.

3. Tax Breaks for Senior Citizens

If you are receiving benefits from US Social Security, Canada Pension Plan (CPP), Quebec Pension Plan (QPP), or Old Age Security (OAS), these receive special tax benefits. At a minimum, 15 percent of your benefit is tax free; if you are a low-income earner, your benefits may be completely free from US tax. Additionally, most states exempt Social Security benefits from tax; some states will also exclude CPP or QPP and OAS benefits.

If you are 65 or older on January 1, you will receive a higher standard deduction, if you do not itemize. For 2012, the standard deduction for a single person 65 or older is $7,400. If you are married filing jointly, the standard deduction is $13,050 if one of you is 65 or older and $14,200 if you are both 65 and older.

4. State Income taxes

In general, you will have to pay state income tax in addition to federal income tax. Forty-one states impose a broad-based income tax on its residents, while seven states (Alaska, Florida, Nevada, South Dakota, Texas, Washington, and Wyoming) have no income tax, and two states (Tennessee and New Hampshire) impose a tax on interest and dividends only.

Caution: You need to consider your total taxes paid such as property (real estate) taxes and sales taxes, not just income taxes. The states with the lowest overall tax burden are Alaska, Nevada, Wyoming, Florida, and Arizona. Notice that Texas, Washington, and Tennessee did not make the list, but Arizona did. The states with the highest overall tax burden are New Jersey, New York, Connecticut, Maryland, Hawaii, and California. (The Resources section at the end of the book has links to all of the states' taxing authorities.)

You may remember that state income tax and property taxes are expenses that are deductible on your federal tax return, if you itemize. However, if you live in a state that chooses to collect tax revenue primarily through sales taxes, you may be out of luck. For tax years through 2011 sales taxes were deductible, but for 2012 and beyond, the law is set to expire unless Congress acts. If you live in a no-income tax state, you could be disadvantaged simply because of how your state chooses to tax its residents.

One thing to consider is that because income taxes are deductible on your federal return and sales taxes are not, you may be better off, financially speaking, living in a low-income tax state such as Tennessee or Arizona than in a state like Florida, because you can deduct the tax you pay. In a very simplistic example, let's say that you pay $100 in sales tax to Florida and you pay $120 in income tax to Arizona. You will be able to deduct the $120 on Schedule A of your federal tax return. If you are in the 25 percent marginal tax bracket, you will lower your federal tax burden by $30 (120 x 25 percent), meaning the Arizona tax cost you $90, net. In this example, you would have been better off by $10, living and paying taxes in Arizona than in Florida.

Planning idea: You have to take your particular circumstances into consideration when determining which state is best for you. Determine the amounts and sources of your income (income tax), your estimated spending (sales tax), and size of home (property tax). From these things, you should be able to get an estimate of the total tax you would pay in each state you are considering; don't forget the after-tax cost of the taxes. Of course you should weigh any tax savings against the lifestyle you want such as proximity to an ocean, airport hub, family, health care, and arts and entertainment.

Another important tax to consider is whether the state has its own estate or inheritance tax. This topic is covered in more detail in

Chapter 10, but keep in mind that 16 states and the District of Columbia have their own estate tax, 6 states have their own inheritance tax, and some states have both. The good news for some of you is that all of the states that impose an estate and/or inheritance tax are in the north, except for Hawaii.

5. Community Property

Community property is a method of holding title (owning) and assets. The reason we bring up community property here is that it can have significant tax-planning implications verses other types of ownership. Not all states allow all possible ways to own a property. In general, there are two types of laws in which to own property, they are called "community property" and "common law."

The states that allow for community property ownership are Arizona, California, Idaho, Louisiana, Nevada, New Mexico, Texas, Washington, and Wisconsin. There are two different ways you can purchase an asset using community property laws; "community property" and "community property with rights of survivorship." In community property states only, married couples can take ownership as community property. In this case, they will each own a half interest in the property. Unlike joint tenants, the owners can pass their interest (half interest) by will or trust upon their death and they will not avoid probate.

Certain community property states allow married couples to own property as community property with rights of survivorship. Similar to community property, the couple will each own a half interest in the property; however, when one of them dies the survivor automatically owns the entire property and avoids the costs and time of probate.

When possible, owning property as community property with rights of survivorship is typically preferable. The reason has to do with income the tax benefits after death. When a couple owns property as joints tenants and one spouse dies, the deceased person's cost basis in his or her half of the property gets adjusted to fair market value (FMV) at the date of death. However, couples owning property as community property with rights of survivorship will have cost basis of the entire (100 percent versus 50 percent) property adjusted to FMV. This means that if there was appreciation in the property at the time of death, the appreciation is completely wiped out when the cost basis is adjusted to FMV at death.

Community property with rights of survivorship is typically preferable to community property without the rights of survivorship because the expenses of probate are avoided. If you recall, the difference between the two forms of community property is that with rights of survivorship, the survivor automatically owns the entire property and avoids probate. Probate is the cost of settling your estate (legal mostly). Any assets that have to be passed to your heirs via your will are subject to probate.

Here is an example of the potential tax benefit:

- John and Carol Smith bought a house for $200,000; meaning that essentially they bought the house for $100,000 each. Five years later John dies when the house is worth $300,000. On the date of death they owned a property worth $150,000 for each of them and each of them had a cost basis of $100,000, giving them each a hypothetical gain of $50,000.

  If the house was bought as joint tenants, only John's half would have its basis adjusted to FMV. This means that the half Carol receives from John has its cost basis adjusted from $100,000 to $150,000. Carol continues to retain her cost basis of $100,000. She now owns the entire property worth $300,000, with a cost basis of $250,000 (Carol's $100,000, plus John's $150,000).

  If the house was bought as community property or as community property with rights of survivorship, both halves would be adjusted at the first death. This means that Carol would inherit the property with a $300,000 cost basis (FMV = $300,000 and basis is adjusted to the FMV). This wipes out all capital gains as of John's death. Carol could sell the property at that time and incur no capital gains.

  Caution: If the property declines in value, the cost basis also declines. In this example, if the property declined to $150,000 at John's death, Carol would inherit the property with a basis of $150,000 — a loss of basis of $50,000. Whereas if they owned the property as joint tenants, the basis would be $175,000 (John's basis is adjusted to half of the FMV and Carol retains her $100,000 basis), leaving a $25,000 capital loss that could be taken if Carol sold the property at that time.

Note: You cannot take a loss on your personal residence.

10

US Estate and Gift Taxes

Up until now, we have discussed only one type of taxation in the United States — the income tax. There is another system of taxation in the US that is imposed on the gratuitous transfer of wealth from one person to another (gift tax), and from one generation to another (estate tax). This system of taxation is collectively called the federal transfer tax system and is composed of three taxes:

- A gift tax that applies to transfers that occur during one's lifetime.

- An estate tax that applies to transfers after death.

- A generation-skipping tax that can occur either during one's lifetime or after death and is applied when one attempts to avoid the gift or estate tax at each generation.

Without the gift tax, you could avoid the estate tax by giving your property away before you die. Without the estate tax, you could avoid the tax by giving all of your property away after you die. Without the generation-skipping tax, you could avoid the tax that would occur at the next generation by transferring your property to a third generation, typically your grandchildren. Therefore, it makes sense that these tax systems are unified in some way. The unification of the federal gift and estate taxes became effective back in 1976, and since that time, they have been sometimes referred to as the federal unified transfer tax system because the same tax rates are used to determine both estate and gift tax liability.

Note: The estate tax laws are in a state of confusion. The law that exists in 2012 is set to expire, and the law that existed in 1996 is scheduled to become the law again in 2013, if Congress does nothing. This would not be that confusing if we knew this would actually happen; however, nearly everyone believes that Congress will pass a law that will, more or less, retain the existing estate tax laws. Therefore, read this chapter for the big picture ideas and check with a cross-border estate planning expert before acting on any of the details in this chapter.

Note: When we talk about spouse throughout this book, we are referring to a heterosexual couple that has been married. At this time, the US (federal government) does not recognize same-sex or common-law marriages. This is true even if the state you live in does recognize these types of marriages.

In Canada, there is no estate tax, but there is a tax on death. Canadians are taxed on the capital gains that arise as a result of the deemed disposition of their capital assets at death. In many circumstances, the deemed disposition tax can be more expensive than the US estate tax because, as you may determine after reviewing this chapter, there are exemptions and credits that often significantly reduce any US estate tax liability. The US estate tax regime is complex, and we suggest that you seek the assistance of a good estate tax attorney and/or accountant whom is well versed in US international estate tax issues, when you are planning or administering an international estate.

We could devote an entire book on the US transfer tax system and how it relates to US citizens, green card holders, and nonresidents. This chapter is meant to be a brief overview of the system to acquaint Canadians on the subject of US estate and gift taxes.

The Internal Revenue Code is analogous to the *Income Tax Act* in Canada; it determines who is subject to transfer taxes using a different set of rules than is used for the income tax system. For income tax purposes, there are US persons (residents or citizens) and nonresident aliens (nonresidents that are also noncitizens). For transfer tax purposes, there are three categories of individuals: US citizens;

US domiciliaries, which are resident aliens; and US non-domiciliaries, which are nonresident aliens.

A green card holder is, by definition, a lawful permanent resident of the US and is therefore taxed as a US resident until the green card is surrendered. This means that if you return to Canada and do not surrender your green card, you continue to be subject to the income-, estate-, and gift-tax laws of the US.

The tests that are used to determine tax residency for income taxes are somewhat different than those tests used to determine residency for transfer taxes. For transfer tax purposes, a concept of "domicile" becomes very important. Having domicile has nothing to do with the number of days you are present in the US. The number of days you are present in the US is the major test for residency, under the income tax rules. Domicile has to do with your intent. Your intent to live and stay in the US indefinitely determines your domicile. The concept of domicile is very subjective, yet very important because if you are deemed to be a US domiciliary, you will be subject to US estate taxes on your worldwide assets.

The IRS does not define the term "domicile" in terms of objective standards. Instead, there are Treasury (the IRS is an organization within the Department of the Treasury) regulations that provide a subjective set of tests based on one's intent to remain indefinitely in the US. The regulations use factors such as the following:

- The duration of stay in the US and other countries.

- The frequency of travel between the US and other countries and between places abroad.

- The size, cost, and nature of the individual's houses or other dwelling places and whether those places are owned or rented.

- The area in which the houses or other dwelling places are located.

- The location of expensive and cherished personal possessions.

- The location of family and close friends.

- The location of the person's church and club memberships and where he or she participates in community activities.

- The location of the any business interests.

- Declarations of residence or intent made in visa or green card applications, wills, deeds, trusts, letters, and other documentation.

- Motivations such as the avoidance of the miseries of war or political regression.

- Visa status.

A noncitizen for income tax purposes may be considered to be a US domiciliary for transfer tax purposes.

The Treaty provides some further guidance and can be used to supersede the IRS rules for determining domicile. It provides that residency for estate tax purposes (domicile) is determined using the same methodology as used under the Treaty, if the deceased taxpayer's estate is relying on the Treaty in calculating the estate tax.

If you are a US citizen or US domiciliary, you will be entitled to a lifetime unified tax credit that can be used to offset US estate and gift taxes. The credit is $1,772,800 and is based on a corresponding applicable estate exclusion of $5.12 million (in 2012). The credit is equivalent to the tax exclusion amount of $5.12 million. Thus, for a US citizen or domiciliary, he or she can have a net taxable estate of up to $5.12 million before any taxes would be incurred. Beginning January 2013, the exclusion amount is schedule to decline to $1,000,000 per person, plus an adjustment for inflation. After being adjusted for inflation, the exclusion is estimated to be approximately $1,300,000.

Beginning in 2011, if you are a US citizen, the amount of exclusion available to you is equal your basic exclusion amount *plus* the unused exclusion of your deceased spouse. The deceased spouse's unused exclusion amount is only available if an election was made on the deceased spouse's estate tax return, United States Estate (and Generation-Skipping Transfer) Tax Return (Form 706). The election can only be made if an estate tax return is filed. So, you may want to file an estate tax return, even if one is not required because the deceased person's estate was not large enough.

The estate tax is calculated on your taxable estate, which is your gross worldwide assets that include the following:

- Life insurance proceeds payable to your estate or, if you owned the policy payable to your heirs.

- The value of certain annuities or pensions payable to your estate or your heirs.

- The value of certain property you transferred out of your estate within the three years before your death.

Less, allowable deductions, which include the following:

- Funeral expenses paid out of your estate.

- Debts you owed at the time of death.

- The value of property passing to your spouse (this is known as the marital deduction and applies to citizens only).

- Charitable deductions made from you estate to a qualified charity (most Canadian charities qualify, but are subject to a limit).

- State death taxes (a small number of states have a separate death tax).

The resulting number is your taxable estate, against which your estate tax is calculated. Once the tax is calculated a credit of up to $1,772,800 is applied. The credit is the tax that would result on a taxable estate of $5,120,000, the exemption for 2012, as noted above.

1. US Nonresident Estate Tax

There are many myths that concern Canadian residents when it comes to US estate tax. One is that the US will tax the Canadian resident on their worldwide estate. The truth is that the US will only tax assets that you own in the US. The other common myth is that the US will take half of everything. The truth is that the estate tax is a flat 35 percent on assets above the exclusion amount. The confusion comes from the fact that the top marginal estate tax rate was 55 percent. Even when the top marginal rate was 55 percent it was still only the tax after the exclusion and after you ran through the lower marginal rates. We discuss below how the nonresident estate tax really works for Canadian residents.

Canadians who are US non-domiciliaries and who own property in the US are subject to US estate tax on certain property deemed to be situated in the US. Under the Internal Revenue Code, the estate of a non-domiciliary, noncitizen of the US is subject to US estate tax only on specific US situs assets that exceed $60,000. Fortunately, the Treaty provides a two-part relief for this. The first relief is afforded through Paragraph 8, Article XXIX B, of the Treaty which provides that, for Canadians with gross estates that are less than US$1.2 million, the tax will only be on the gains of real property situated in the US and personal property that forms a part of a US business. The second relief comes from Paragraph 2 of Article XXIX B which grants a pro-rata unified credit to the estate of a Canadian resident decedent for purposes of computing US estate tax. The allowed pro-rata credit is determined by multiplying the US estate tax credit of $1,772,800 ($5,120,000 exemption of assets in 2012) by a fraction, the numerator of which is the value of the part of the gross estate situated in the US and the denominator of which is the value of the entire gross estate wherever situated.

In other words, a nonresident can generally have up to $60,000 of US assets before he or she would be subject to US estate taxes. However, the Treaty can be used to increase the $60,000 exemption by providing Canadians who are nonresidents and noncitizens of the US with a proportionate allocation of the $5,120,000 exemption allowed US citizens and domiciliaries. The exemption can never be less than the $60,000, so for smaller estates, a person can use the $60,000 exemption, allowed for under the Internal Revenue Code. For larger estates, a Canadian nonresident of the US can use the Treaty formula of US assets divided by worldwide assets, times $5,120,000.

For example, a Canadian resident and US nonresident and noncitizen, owns a condo in Arizona worth $250,000. That person has a worldwide net worth, including life insurance, of $1,500,000. That means that about 17 percent of the person's assets are in the US and he or she can use 17 percent of the $5,120,000 exemption, or $870,400. Since the exemption ($870,400) is greater than the amount of assets in the US ($250,000), there is no US estate tax.

The estate of the person in the example above would have to file an estate tax return even though there is no estate tax due. Since the Treaty allowed for the extra exclusion, not US tax law, an estate tax return must be filed to make an election to invoke the Treaty provision. Without the benefit of the Treaty, the exemption would have been limited to $60,000. However, if the value of US assets is equal to, or less than $60,000, no return would have to be filed.

How do you determine what constitutes US assets, also known as US "situs property"? The rules for determining US situs property for a nonresident, non-US citizen are determined under the laws of the Internal Revenue Code; the treaty does not provide guidance in determining what does or does not constitute US situs property. US situs property includes personal property normally located in the US and includes such things as vehicles, jewelry, artwork, boats, RVs, furniture, and collectibles. Shares of US corporations, regardless of where they were purchased or where they are physically held and certain bonds and notes issued by US residents and corporations are also included, even if those securities are held in Canadian registered accounts. This includes shares of mutual funds and electronically traded funds issued by US companies. It does not include American Depository Receipts of foreign corporations, which are shares of foreign corporations listed on a US stock exchange. It includes interests in certain trusts if the assets in the trust have US situs. It also includes any business-related assets owned by a sole proprietor and used in a US business. Bequests to charitable organizations in the US reduce the US situs property.

Assets normally excluded from the numerator of the formula used for a nonresident include US bank deposits, proceeds of life insurance on the life of the decedent, and shares or notes of non-US corporations. In general, if interest from a debt instrument to a nonresident of the US is exempt from US taxation, the underlying debt obligation is likely to be excluded from the US estate. Code Section 2104(e) provides that the rule of estate tax inclusion does not apply to a debt obligation where interest would be treated as income from sources outside of the US for income tax purposes.

Neither the US income tax code nor the regulations specifically address the situs of partnership interests for estate tax purposes, and case law and rulings are inconclusive. It is reasonable to conclude that a nonresident alien's interest in a US partnership, particularly if it is engaged in a US trade or business, will be included as US situs property.

Deductions for expenses and debts of a nonresident's US estate are allowed, but only in proportion to the value of the US estate to the worldwide estate. For example, if the deceased nonresident has an outstanding loan for $30,000, and the US estate (not including the deduction for the loan) is $500,000 and is part of a worldwide estate of $1,000,000, then 50 percent of the loan would be deducted from the US estate. There is, in effect, an exception for real property encumbered by nonrecourse indebtedness. Because the debt is non-recourse, if the real property is included in the US estate, then the entire indebtedness can be deducted.

All of the US estate property is combined, net of the calculation of encumbrances on the property, and is used as the numerator in the estate tax calculation for a nonresident Canadian in the US.

The denominator is the US non-domiciliary's worldwide estate (or the "gross estate"). The IRS sets the rules for determining what is included in the nonresident's worldwide estate. IRS Code Section 2031 defines the gross estate of a decedent as including "all property, real or personal, tangible or intangible, wherever situated." It includes all of the assets that were used in the numerator of the formula, and it also includes interests in corporations, life insurance proceeds, and bank deposits including checking, savings, money market accounts, Guaranteed Investment Certificates (GICs), and Certificate of Deposits (CDs).

It includes the full value of Canadian-controlled private corporations which you control or have controlled and in which you still own shares, and the present value of all future payments you might leave to a spouse under the spousal benefit of your pension plan.

All investment accounts and all stocks and bonds owned in certificate form are included. Retirement accounts are included, such as US Individual Retirement Accounts (IRAs) and 401(k)s. It includes Canadian mutual funds, Canadian Registered Retirement Savings Plans, and Exchange-Traded Funds (ETFs).

Funeral expenses, administration expenses, debts, and claims against the estate are fully deductible from the gross estate. If property is located in a state that has a state death tax, there is an allowable deduction for any state taxes that you may incur from the federal gross estate. Charitable deductions made to either Canadian charities or US charities are deductible from the gross estate.

There is a special elective "marital credit" allowed by paragraph 3 of Article XXIX B of the Treaty for Canadian nonresidents. This credit is available for property that is transferred to a spouse who is a US or Canadian resident or a citizen of the US. The credit provides that the property transferred to a spouse will be credited against the deceased spouse's gross estate (the denominator) and the US estate (the numerator). The credit that is allowed is the lesser of the unified tax credit and the US estate tax that would otherwise be imposed on the property. Thus, for most married Canadians who own property in the US, an estate tax would not become due until the death of the second spouse.

The treaty provides relief to a double taxation issue that, not so long ago, had been problematic for Canadians and US persons who owned property in both countries. For a nonresident of the US who owns property that is subject to US estate taxes or has a taxable US estate given the rules described above, any taxes incurred in the US either for US federal or state estate or inheritance taxes may be credited toward taxes paid in Canada on the same property for capital gains resulting from deemed disposition that occurs upon death. In other words, a foreign tax credit may be claimed against Canadian income tax otherwise payable on US source income on the deceased's final Canadian tax return.

2. US Resident, Noncitizen Estate Tax

Generally, resident aliens in the US are afforded nearly identical estate tax treatment as US citizens, with certain exceptions. The Internal Revenue Code imposes a federal estate tax on the taxable estate of every decedent who is a resident or citizen of the US. The gross estate of each citizen or resident includes his or her worldwide property. The value of property which passes from a decedent to a surviving spouse who is a US citizen is deducted as a "marital credit" from the decedent's gross estate.

The tentative estate tax owed is determined by multiplying the taxable estate by the appropriate rate tables, and in 2012 the highest marginal tax rate is 35 percent. Table 15 provides the unified transfer tax rates for gifts made and for deaths before applicable credits. The tentative tax is reduced by the unified tax credit. As mentioned earlier in this chapter, the unified tax credit is unified with both the estate tax and the gift tax. To prevent estate tax revenue loss through lifetime transfers, the gift tax system imposes a tax on inter vivos gratuitous transfers (i.e., made during one's lifetime). The unified tax credit that is remaining to be used in the estate tax calculation is net of taxes paid during a person's lifetime. Gift taxes will be discussed in section **3.**

Table 15
GIFT AND ESTATE TAX RATE SCHEDULE

2010 – 2012 Gift and Estate Tax Rate Schedule	Tentative Tax Equals		
Taxable Estate	Base Tax	Plus	Of Amount Over
0 – $10,000	$0	18%	$0
$10,000 – $20,000	$1,800	20%	$10,000
$20,000 – $40,000	$3,800	22%	$20,000
$40,000 – $60,000	$8,200	24%	$40,000
$60,000 – $80,000	$13,000	26%	$60,000
$80,000 – $100,000	$18,200	28%	$80,000
$100,000 – $150,000	$23,800	30%	$100,000
$150,000 – $250,000	$38,800	32%	$150,000
$250,000 – $500,000	$70,800	34%	$250,000
$500,000+	$155,000	35%	$500,000
Credit shelter amount $5,000,000 in 2011, $5,120,000 in 2012	**Credit amount $1,730,800 in 2011, $1,772,800 in 2012**		

Under the *Economic Growth and Tax Relief Reconciliation Act* (EGTRRA) of 2001, the estate and gift unified tax credit (and the corresponding exclusion amount) has varied wildly over the past ten-plus years, starting at a credit of $192,800 based on an exclusion of $600,000 in 2000, and increasing progressively until the estate tax was repealed for the year 2010. It was then reinstated based on a $5 million exclusion in 2011 that was increased, because of inflation, to $5.12 million per person, in 2012. Table 16 includes the unified tax credits and the corresponding exclusion amounts since 2001.

Not only have the unified tax credits and exclusion amounts varied, the tax rates and brackets have varied as well. At the end of 2012, barring Congressional action, the unified exclusion amount will revert back to $1 million per person with a top marginal tax rate of 55 percent. The $1 million dollars will be adjusted for inflation since 2000, and will end up being around $1.3 million after adjusting for inflation. Many people are holding their breath waiting for Congress to act, and most experts agree that there will be adjustments to these limits sometime in early 2013.

Table 16
UNIFIED TAX CREDITS AND EXCLUSION AMOUNTS

Year	Applicable Unified Tax Credit Amount	Applicable Exclusion Amount	Top Federal Estate Tax Rate
2001	$220,550	$650,000	55%
2002	$345,800	$1,000,000	50%
2003	$345,800	$1,000,000	49%
2004	$555,800	$1,500,000	48%
2005	$555,800	$1,500,000	47%
2006	$780,800	$2,000,000	46%
2007	$780,800	$2,000,000	45%
2008	$780,800	$2,000,000	45%
2009	$1,245,800	$3,500,000	45%
2010	No Federal Estate Tax		
2011	$1,730,800	$5,000,000	35%
2012	$1,772,800	$5,120,000	35%

While citizens and resident aliens are similarly subject to the estate tax, there are important distinctions that relate to citizenship. Direct gifts and direct bequests by a decedent to a noncitizen spouse do not qualify for the unlimited marital deduction. As part of this provision, gifts in trust that would otherwise qualify for a marital deduction will not qualify when the spouse is not a citizen. That is unless the trust meets certain requirements as a Qualified Domestic Trust (QDOT). A marital deduction is allowed if the property transfers to a QDOT.

There are two other circumstances when a marital deduction would be allowed for a noncitizen spouse of a decedent. The deduction is allowed if the surviving spouse becomes a US citizen before the decedent's estate tax return is filed and has maintained US residency at all times after the decedent's death and until becoming a US citizen. The deduction is also allowed for property passing directly to the surviving spouse if the surviving spouse irrevocably transfers the assets to a QDOT before filing the decedent's estate tax return.

Most estate plans in the US for married couples with noncitizen spouses include QDOT provisions. A QDOT is a statutorily defined trust that permits married couples with at least one noncitizen spouse to take advantage of the marital deduction. The QDOT does not eliminate the estate tax; it merely postpones the tax until the death of the surviving spouse or other subsequent taxable event. The post-poned tax always remains that of the first decedent spouse. A surviving spouse's applicable exclusion amount cannot be used to shelter QDOT assets from estate tax. Also, the QDOT tax remains equal to the tax that would have been imposed if the amount involved in the taxable event had been included in the first decedent's estate — at the tax rate that was in effect at the decedent's death.

Note: The primary difference between the unlimited marital deduction allowed to a US-citizen spouse and the unlimited deferral to a non-US citizen spouse using a QDOT is that assets passed to a US citizen can be consumed before death and never have to be included in the surviving spouse's estate. If that happened, there would be no tax due on those assets in the surviving spouse's estate. With a QDOT, however, there is no chance of that; any distributions of principal from the QDOT triggers an estate tax.

The QDOT is designed to ensure that the property held in the trust will be subject to US federal estate tax, and the noncitizen spouse cannot flee the US with the assets and avoid taxation. The QDOT can be created by the deceased spouse's executor post death or by the noncitizen surviving spouse to hold property he or she received outright from the decedent.

For a US tax resident or citizen who owns Canadian property, there is certain Canadian property that will become taxable in Canada at his or her death as a deemed disposition of capital assets. When a nonresident of Canada dies holding Taxable Canadian Property (TCP) the CRA deems the nonresident to have disposed of all of his or her TCP immediately prior to death for proceeds equal to the fair market value of the TCP at the date of death. TCP includes real property located in Canada, Canadian business property used in a business in Canada, or any stock owned in companies which have a significant portion of their fair market value in real property.

Because the US includes worldwide assets in the gross estate for US estate tax purposes, TCP will not only be taxed at death in Canada, it will also be part of the US gross estate. Under Paragraph 7 of Article XXIXB of the treaty, the US will allow a credit for Canadian deemed disposition taxes paid against US federal estate tax imposed on the Canadian property included in the estate of a US resident or US citizen, or upon the death of the surviving spouse holding a QDOT. The credit is allowed for any Canadian federal and provincial income taxes imposed at death as a result of property of the estate that was located outside of the US.

2.1 Jointly held property

The rules surrounding jointly held property become very complicated. Simply, the Code Section 2056(d)(1)(B) states that property owned jointly with right of survivorship between spouses will be included at one-half of its value in the estate of the first to die. This does not apply if the surviving spouse of the decedent is not a US citizen. Instead, 100 percent of the property is includable in the first decedent's estate except to the extent the executor can substantiate the contributions of the noncitizen spouse to the acquisition of the property. Jointly owned US situs property will be fully includable in the estate of a nonresident alien who provided the funds to buy the property. Because jointly owned property with a right of survivorship passes outright to the surviving spouse, if the surviving spouse is not a US citizen, the surviving spouse will need to transfer the portion included in the estate to a QDOT in order to qualify for the marital deduction.

Joint ownership does not mean the same thing in the US as it does in Canada, so we recommend that you seek legal advice regarding titling and ownership of your US property.

3. Gift Taxes

US gift tax is imposed on taxable gifts (i.e., total gifts less exclusions and deductions) made by US citizens, US domiciliaries, and non-US domiciliaries. The treaty does not provide any provisions for inter vivos gifts (i.e., transfers made during a person's lifetime). The rules for transfer taxes and filing requirements for lifetime gifts are dictated from US Internal Revenue Code. The gift tax system is laden with rules, exceptions, and exemptions.

Transfers from US citizens and domiciliaries are subject to gift tax on all transfers of property, regardless of where the property is located. Alternatively, non-US domiciliaries are only subject to US gift tax on transfers of real property and tangible personal property situated in the US. Gifts of intangible property, which includes stocks and bonds regardless of where they are located, made by a non-US domiciliary are not subject to US gift tax.

Transfers to spouses have gifting rules that are unique from gifting rules to non-spouses. To determine what tax consequences result from a lifetime gift, it is helpful to look at the direction the assets are flowing. If there is a transfer between spouses, and the flow is to a US citizen, then the transfer is generally free from any tax consequences and there is no limit on the amount that can be transferred. However, if the flow is to a noncitizen spouse, the tax law guards against that person's leaving the country and avoiding the US government's ability to tax the individual. For this reason, there are limits on transfers of US property that can be made to noncitizen spouses, whether or not they are resident aliens or nonresident aliens of the US. For a taxpayer with a noncitizen spouse, IRC Section 2523(i)(2) allows a $139,000 (2012) annual exclusion on gifts to a noncitizen spouse, which means he or she can only transfer assets to a noncitizen spouse of up to $139,000 per year. This can be problematic for married couples in creating joint gifts. As an example, assume a couple has moved from Canada to the US and is purchasing real property in the US. The money to purchase the property is coming from the husband's personal account. The wife is not a US citizen. This will result in a gift to the wife equal to 50 percent of the value of the transfer amount, and if that gift exceeds $139,000, then there will be a taxable gift, and a gift tax return must be filed and gift tax will be due. The current marginal rate on gift and estate tax is 35 percent (the unified tax rate).

A more complicated example is what seems, at first blush, to be a harmless transaction. Instead of purchasing real property, the couple creates a joint bank account funded from an account owned by the husband only; this too is a joint gift. However, the creation of a joint bank account is treated differently from other joint gifts because the gift is not completed until the non-contributing party — the wife in this example — withdraws money for her own benefit. The reasoning is simple: The contributing party (the husband) could withdraw the money and use it for his own purposes because both spouses have access to the funds. In transactions involving joint bank accounts, a gift occurs only upon withdrawal by the non-contributing party for her benefit.

For gifts to anyone other than one's spouse, any person can make an annual gift of $13,000 (2012) per donee to anyone, at no transfer tax cost, a long as the gift is of a present interest. All individuals, whether they are resident in the US or not, can gift, transfer-tax free, up to $13,000 per year to any donee (the $13,000 is referred to as the "annual exclusion amount" and is indexed annually for inflation). For spouses, gift splitting is available; which means that one spouse can be the donor but use the other spouse's annual exclusion amount. However, if either spouse is a US non-domiciliary, gift splitting is not permitted. A gift can be a gift of a present interest or a gift of a future interest, and only present interest gifts will qualify for the annual exclusion. A present interest is an unrestricted right to the immediate use of the property.

Many Canadian residents, as well as US citizens and residents, who own property in the US, may want to add their adult children to the title of the property. If you are a Canadian resident and already own the US property, and you do not receive payment from the children for the value of their proportionate ownership of the property, there will be both Canadian and US tax implications. First, the CRA will consider this transfer subject to capital gains tax on the portion of the property being transferred. The IRS will consider the transfer of the US property as a gift. If you are a Canadian resident, however, and you do not yet own the property, you may be able to add children or other owners to the title as you wish without gift tax implications. For US residents and US citizens, adding the names of your children or other persons to the title would be considered a gift for US gift tax purposes unless market value consideration is paid for the assignment of ownership.

4. Generation Skipping Transfer Tax

We briefly want to mention the generation skipping transfer tax which is part of the transfer tax regime. This tax is imposed on transfers to unrelated persons who are more than 37.5 years younger than the donor or to related persons who are more than one generation younger than the donor, such as grandchildren and great grandchildren (known as "skip persons"). This additional tax applies to gifts made during one's lifetime or bequests in an estate. The tax prevents someone from skipping tax on a generation by gifting directly to the next generation. Gifts to skip persons are taxed at basically double the unified tax rate for gifts and estates. There are exemptions, exclusions, and credits that follow similar rules to those for gifts and estates.

5. State Estate and Inheritance Tax

Just because you fall under the federal exemption of $5,120,000, does not necessarily mean you will not pay an estate or inheritance tax at death. As of this writing, 17 states and the District of Columbia have their own estate tax. Eight states have an inheritance tax and three states have both.

By this point you know what an estate tax is, but you are wondering what an inheritance tax is. An inheritance tax is imposed by states on the inheritors (beneficiaries) of the assets. All states that impose an inheritance tax allow assets to be transferred to a spouse tax free. Some states, but not all, allow assets to go to the children tax free. All states but one has a zero or nominal exemption from the tax, meaning that virtually every dollar is taxed; Tennessee has a $1 million exemption. See Table 17.

Table 17
STATE ESTATE AND INHERITANCE TAX

State	Estate Tax (Exemption)	Inheritance Tax Percent
Alabama	N/A	
Alaska	N/A	
Arizona	N/A	
Arkansas	N/A	
California	N/A	
Colorado	N/A	
Connecticut	$2,000,000	
Delaware	$5,120,000	
District of Columbia	$1,000,000	
Florida	N/A	
Georgia	N/A	
Hawaii	$3,600,000	
Idaho	N/A	
Illinois	$3,500,000	
Indiana	N/A	Yes (1% to 20%)
Iowa	N/A	Yes (5% to 15%)

Kansas	N/A	
Kentucky	N/A	Yes (4% to 16%)
Louisiana	N/A	
Maine	$1,000,000	
Maryland	$1,000,000	Yes (10%)
Massachusetts	$1,000,000	
Michigan	N/A	
Minnesota	$1,000,000	
Mississippi	N/A	
Missouri	N/A	
Montana	N/A	
Nebraska	N/A	Yes (1% to 18%)
Nevada	N/A	
New Hampshire	N/A	
New Jersey	$675,000	Yes (0% to 16 %)
New Mexico	N/A	
New York	$1,000,000	
North Carolina	$5,120,000	
North Dakota	N/A	
Ohio	$338,333	
Oklahoma	N/A	
Oregon	$1,000,000	
Pennsylvania	N/A	Yes (4.5% to 15%)
Rhode Island	$892,865	
South Carolina	N/A	
South Dakota	N/A	
Tennessee	$1,000,000	Yes (9.5%)
Texas	N/A	
Utah	N/A	
Vermont	$2,750,000	
Virginia	N/A	
Washington	$2,000,000	

West Virginia	N/A	
Wisconsin	N/A	
Wyoming	N/A	

It should be clear to you by now that the international estate tax rules should not be taken lightly, and it is essential when dealing with an estate with both US and Canadian property, you should seek professional advice from an expert in this field. We covered the basics of the US estate tax implications, but our discussion merely brushed the surface of the issues that could be encountered in a multi-national estate. Furthermore, more than just tax implications need to considered such as estate, trust, and probate laws that must be adhered to for the proper administration of an estate. Note that the international estate waters are deep and treacherous.

11

Leaving the US

There can be many reasons for leaving the US; returning to Canada from a temporary work assignment, your family situation changes, or you simply don't like living in the US. Regardless of the reason, there will most likely be tax ramifications to your move back to Canada. From a tax perspective, there are three broad categories that people fall into when leaving the US and each has a different tax ramification. The categories are US citizens, long-term permanent residents (green card holders), and anyone that is neither a US citizen nor a long-term green card holder.

The easiest category, from a tax perspective, includes those people that are not US citizens and are not long-term green card holders. Before leaving the US, all aliens (non-US citizens) are required to obtain a Certificate of Compliance (also known as a "sailing permit"). To get a Certificate of Compliance, you must go to a local IRS office between two and four weeks before leaving the US. You must file either the US Departing Alien Income Tax Statement (Form 2063 — short form) or the US Departing Alien Income Tax Return (Form 1040-C — long form) and take it with you to an IRS office to obtain a clearance certificate. The certificate cannot be issued more than 30 days before you leave. If you are married, you each must receive a clearance certificate, therefore you and your spouse must each file one of the forms and go to the IRS office.

Form 2063 is the short form that asks for basic information, but does not compute the tax due. Those that qualify for using the short form are people who have filed a least one tax return (and paid tax, if applicable) in the US, and are people who —

- had no taxable income during the year up to the date of departure; or

- have taxable income during the year or preceding year and "whose departure will not hinder the collection of any tax." If the IRS has information indicating that the person is leaving to avoid paying tax, he or she must file Form 1040-C and pay the tax.

Examples of aliens not required to obtain a Certificate of Compliance are diplomats, students, those receiving no taxable income, and alien residents of Canada or Mexico who commute and have wages that are subject to withholding.

We strongly recommend that you call two or more months ahead to schedule an appointment. It will likely be very difficult to find an IRS agent that will know what to do when you call for an appointment. Calling ahead will give you and the agent time to find someone who knows what to do, or at least will spend the time to learn what to do.

1. Expatriation

US citizens and lawful permanent residents (green card holders) are required to report and pay tax on their worldwide income, regardless of where they reside. To remove yourself from the US tax system, you must give up your citizenship or green card and become a nonresident alien. If you are a US citizen who wants to become a nonresident alien, you must renounce your citizenship and move to another country.

An expatriation tax applies to US citizens that renounced their citizenship and long-term residents who have ended their residency. A long-term resident is defined as someone who has been a green card holder for at least 8 of the last 15 years prior to expatriation.

If you are deciding whether you should become a US citizen, we would say that if you have the opportunity, you should become a US citizen, unless you do not believe citizenship will be permanent. No one should be a citizen of any country unless they believe it will be permanent. However, circumstances can change and the issue of renouncing your US citizenship may come up in the future. Note that there is no income tax difference between a citizen and a long-term green card holder, before, during, or after expatriation.

The advantages of citizenship over being a green card holder include the following:

- Estate tax advantage: US citizens are allowed to receive unlimited assets from their spouse (traditional marriage), without the deceased spouse paying US estate tax at his or her death.

- The right to vote in elections.

- Protection or assistance by the government when overseas.

The following are the benefits of a green card holder:

- Easier to give up citizenship, if that time ever comes.

- It is possible to relinquish and reacquire green card status, where it is impossible to reacquire citizenship if it surrendered.

You are considered to have relinquished your US citizenship on the *earliest* of the following dates:

- The date you renounce your US citizenship before a diplomatic or consular officer of the US, assuming the renouncement was later confirmed by the issuance of a Certificate of Loss of Nationality of the United States.

- The date you furnished to the State Department a signed statement of your voluntary relinquishment of US nationality confirming the performance of an expatriating act, providing the voluntary relinquishment was later confirmed by the issuance of a Certificate of Loss of Nationality of the United States.

- The date the State Department issues a Certificate of Loss of Nationality of the United States.

- The date a US court canceled your Certificate of US Naturalization.

If you are a long-term resident that is terminating your residency, it will be on the *earliest* of the following dates:

- The date you file the Department of Homeland Security Abandonment of Lawful Permanent Resident Status (Form I-407) with a US consular or immigration officer, and Homeland Security has determined that you have in fact, abandoned your lawful permanent resident status.

- The date you became subject to a final administrative order for your removal from the US under the *Immigration and Nationality Act*, and you have actually left the US as a result of that order.

- If you were a dual resident of the US and a country with which the US has an income tax treaty (e.g., Canada), the date you commenced to be treated as a resident of that country and you determined that, for purposes of the treaty, you are a resident of the treaty country and gave notice to the Secretary of such treatment.

Although a person that expatriates will be treated as a nonresident alien, he or she may be classified as a "covered expatriate," which would subject the person to an exit tax, similar to the tax Canada imposes on its residents when they leave Canada and become residents of another country. The exit tax imposes an immediate tax, as well as potential future taxes on the expatriate. A covered expatriate is either a US citizen or long-term resident who abandons or loses his or her status as a US citizen or permanent resident, and as of the day before expatriation has —

- an average net income tax for the last five years that is more than $151,000 (2012);

- a net worth on the date of expatriation that is $2 million or more; or

- failed to certify, under penalty of perjury, that he or she has complied with all US federal tax obligations for the five years preceding the date of his or her expatriation or termination of residency. Certification is done using the Initial and Annual Expatriation Statement (Form 8854). This form is completed when filing Form 1040 (or 1040NR) for the year of expatriation.

The income tax amount of $151,000 is increased for cost-of-living adjustments each year. There is no adjustment for the net worth amount of $2 million.

Note: The $151,000 amount is the tax, not the income. This means that if you assume an average or effective tax rate of 30 percent, you need more than $500,000 of taxable income (not gross income). This seems like a much higher threshold than $2 million net worth, so the vast majority of those expatriating will be considered a covered expatriate due to having a net worth in excess of $2 million.

If you expatriate and you are considered a covered expatriate, you will be subject to a mark-to-market tax, also known as a "deemed disposition of your worldwide assets," and will be required to recognize gain on those assets as if they were sold at their fair market value, as of the day prior to your expatriation.

If you are a long-term resident, you have the option of using the fair market value of you assets on the day your US residency began. For the assets you owned when you moved to the US, this will, in most cases, be a higher number and therefore produce a lower gain than using the original purchase price.

There are three groups of assets that are not subject to the mark-to-market tax, but will be taxed using a different method: deferred compensation, tax-deferred accounts, and an interest in a non-grantor trust. If you have one or more of these types of accounts, you must file a Notice of Expatriation and Waiver of Treaty Benefits (Form W-8CE) within 30 days of expatriation. (For more detailed information regarding the mark-to-market regime, refer to Notice 2009-85.)

Deferred compensation is divided into two types:

- The US payor is required to withhold on all payments.

- All other deferred compensation arrangements.

Where US withholding is required, payment can be deferred until payment is made, but the withholding must be 30 percent. The covered expatriate cannot claim, under the Treaty, to reduce the withholding. For all other deferred compensation arrangements, the accrued benefit will be treated as being received the day before expatriation. Examples of deferred compensation plans include a company pension or profit-sharing plan (including 401(k) and 403(b) accounts), simplified employee pensions (SEP), and simplified retirement accounts (SIMPLE plans).

Important: Any interests in a foreign pension or retirement account are considered deferred compensation plans and are included in the expatriation tax. This includes your RRSPs, RRIFs, LIRAs, any Canadian company pension, government, or military pension, but does not include Canadian Pension Plan (CPP) or Old Age Security (OAS), which are forms of social security.

Tax deferred accounts are individual retirement plans, a qualified tuition plan (i.e., Section 529 Plan), a Coverdell Education Savings Account, a health savings account, and an Archer MSA. However, SEP and SIMPLE plans of a covered expatriate are treated as deferred compensation items. These plans are treated as if the entire interest was paid out on the day prior to expatriation.

The definition of a non-grantor trust is a trust occurs when the grantor gives the control of the trust property to a trustee other than himself or herself. In other words, a non-grantor trust is a trust that someone established for the benefit of someone other than himself or herself.

So, if someone (e.g., your parents) established a trust in which you are the beneficiary, or at least one of the beneficiaries, the value of your share of the trust is subject to the expatriation tax. If you are the beneficiary of such a trust, the trustee must withhold 30 percent of any direct or indirect distributions. This withholding rule applies to both domestic (US) and foreign (non-US) trusts.

There are two exceptions from the automatic treatment of the tax described above. The first is for a dual-citizen who became a US citizen at birth and must have also become a citizen of the other country at birth; or the person was a resident of the US for 10 years or less, out of the last 15, prior to the year in which the expatriation occurred. This refers to naturalized citizens (those that went through the process of becoming a US citizen).

The second exception is for minors, if *all* of the following conditions are met:

- The person became a US citizen at birth.
- Expatriation occurs before attaining age 18.5.
- The person was not a US resident for more than ten years before expatriation occurs.

If you are subject to the expatriate tax regime, the US provides an exemption from tax in amount of $651,000 (2012 and indexed for inflation). This means that many of you will not owe tax upon expatriating. If your gain is greater than $651,000, you pay tax on the difference.

You can make an irrevocable election to defer the payment of the tax. If you make the election, the following rules apply.

- You must make the election on a property-by-property basis.

- The deferred tax on a particular property is due on the return for the tax year in which you dispose of the property.

- Interest is charged for the period the tax is deferred.

- The due date for the payment of the deferred tax cannot be extended beyond the earlier of the following dates:

  - The due date of the return required for the year of death.

  - The time that the security provided for the property fails to be adequate (see the next point).

- You must provide adequate security, such as a bond.

- You must make an irrevocable waiver of any right under any treaty of the US that would preclude assessment or collection of any tax imposed under this expatriation regime.

- You must file the Initial and Annual Expatriation Statement (Form 8854) annually for each year, up to and including, the year in which the full amount of deferred tax and interest is paid.

The consequence of being in the US for more than 30 days, in any calendar year, after expatriation is that you will be treated as a US citizen for tax purposes and taxed on your worldwide income. This rule will apply for the longer of ten years or until the full amount of deferred tax and interest is paid. There is one exception to this rule. You can be in the US for up to 60 days without being treated as a US citizen if either of the following requirements is met:

- You were performing personal services in the US for an employer who is not related to you, and you meet these additional requirements:

  You were a US citizen and, within a reasonable period of time following your expatriation, you became a citizen or resident, fully liable to tax in the country in which you, your spouse, or either of your parents were born.

For each year, in the 10 years prior to your expatriation, you were physically present in the US for 30 days or less.

Form 8854 must be filed upon the date of renunciation with the American Citizens Services Unit, Consular Section, of the nearest American Embassy or consulate.

In addition to the information discussed above, the following information is required:

- Taxpayer's identification number (Social Security number)
- Mailing address of the principal foreign residence
- Expatriation date
- Foreign country in which you are residing
- Foreign country or countries of which you are a citizen and the date you became a citizen of those foreign countries
- Information detailing your income, assets, and liabilities
- Number of days during any portion of which you were physically present in the US during the taxable year
- How you became a US citizen (birth or naturalization)

A helpful resource is the Renunciation website (renunciation-guide.com/Renunciation-Process-Step-By-Step.html). This site was established by a couple of people that renounced citizenship, so they have real world experiences to share with you. It is not a government site and we have not verified the information on the site, so we suggest that you double check any information you receive from the site.

1.1 Your rights after renunciation of US citizenship

After your renunciation, you will have the same rights in the US as any other citizen of Canada or whatever country you are a citizen of.

If you renounce your citizenship when you expatriate, you will lose the following rights in the US:

- You lose the right to live and work in the US.
- You will not be able to vote in US elections.

- You will not be entitled to the protection of the US overseas.

- You will no longer be able to enter, and remain indefinitely, in the US.

- Any children you have who are born after your renunciation will not receive US citizenship from you (although they may receive US citizenship from the other parent, from birth on US soil, or from naturalization later in life).

There are no temporary renunciations or options to reacquire US citizenship. Renunciation of US citizenship is irrevocable; you lose your citizenship for the rest of your life. In contrast, a British citizen is allowed to renounce his or her citizenship in order to acquire another nationality, and then later reapply for and "resume" his or her British citizenship at a future date. In the US, there is no such provision. Once you renounce, you can never resume your citizenship.

After your renunciation, your biometric information (i.e., ten-digit fingerprints and digital photograph) will be taken and stored by the US either when you apply for a visa or when you enter the US. This policy applies to all non-US citizens from the ages of 14 to 79.

1.2 The Reed Amendment

The only law that calls for different treatment is the Reed Amendment. In 1996, Congress included a provision in the expatriation law to bar entry to any individual "who officially renounces United States citizenship and who is determined by the Attorney General to have renounced United States citizenship for the purpose of avoiding taxation by the United States."

This section of the 1996 immigration law, known as the Reed Amendment, added ex-citizens to the list of other "inadmissibles" which includes practicing polygamists, international child abductors, and aliens who have unlawfully voted in US elections. However, to date the Reed Amendment has never been imposed.

So while in theory, it's possible that the US could bar you from entry to the US because the Attorney General believes you expatriated with the primary purpose of avoiding US taxation, we think the chances are extremely low that this would ever happen under current law.

2. Tax Planning before You Leave

Most of you will not be subject to the expatriation tax, but you should still have tax planning done before you leave to maximize your planning opportunities; once you leave the US a number of planning options will no longer be available. In fact, the best tax-planning opportunities exist only while you are still a US taxpayer.

We recommend reading Robert Keats' book, *The Border Guide* before moving to Canada. Mr. Keats devotes an entire chapter on the subject of moving to Canada. Also, *The Taxation of Americans in Canada* is scheduled to print in 2013. If you are an American or Canadian who is retaining a green card, this book will discuss the Canadian and US tax laws that you will need to comply with.

Because a complete discussion of this topic is outside of the scope of this book, we will only highlight some of the issues to consider before leaving the US:

- What should you do with your savings and non-qualified (non-registered) accounts in the US?

- What should you do with your qualified (registered) accounts in the US?

- If you still have registered accounts (e.g., RRSPs) in Canada, should you cash them out before returning?

- What should you do with your home in the US? If you do not sell it before leaving, what are the tax consequences?

- If you have entities such as US corporations or partnerships, what should you do with them?

- If applicable, what should you do regarding social security and/or Medicare?

- If you are not a US citizen, should a pre-immigration trust be used?

As we explained before, we recommend talking to a cross-border tax specialist to get these questions and any other questions answered before you leave the US.

Conclusion

We have attempted to present a topic that has never been presented before in such depth. As the trailblazers, we had no path to follow so we hope that the path we chose was both helpful and at least somewhat interesting. The challenges were trying to find the right balance between too much and not enough information, and how to present a fundamentally boring subject in a way that would at least make it readable. We hope that we overcame both challenges and that you will find this book a useful resource.

From a content perspective, our intent was to share what we have learned over more the 20 years of specializing in US-Canada tax and financial planning. While some chapters such as the basics of US taxation could have been written by most US tax professionals, most of the chapters are filled with unique insights only a few people could provide. We gladly share this information and hope that you benefit from what you learn.

Now that you have read through the book, you no doubt have questions that were not answered or were not explained clearly enough. Please feel free to give us your suggestions so that we can incorporate them into the next edition of the book. As professionals, we always want to do a good job and are constantly looking to improve; your comments will help to make this book as good as it can be.

This book is only information; it is not a substitute for qualified professional advice. Just as you would not consider reading a book on foot surgery then attempting to operate on your foot, you should not expect that you can learn everything there is to know about the taxation of Canadians living in the US in this book.

We know from experience that some of you will call or email us with questions. While we sincerely would like to help you (that is why we are in this business), please understand that we will not be able to get to all of your questions. While we will occasionally answer questions for free, we are in the business of giving valuable advice for a fee.

Lastly, we want to remind you that if you found this book useful, we have other books that you might also be interested in. All of the books can be ordered by calling our office; from the publisher, Self-Counsel Press; our websites, and from Amazon.

- *The Border Guide: A Guide to Living, Working and Investing across the Border*, by Robert Keats

- *A Canadian's Best Tax Haven: The US*, by Robert Keats

- *Buying Real Estate in the US: The Concise Guide for Canadians*, by Dale Walters

Don't forget that we will have a new book published in 2013 called the *Taxation of Americans in Canada*.

Resources:
Contact Information for State Taxing Agencies

State	State Tax Authority Website	Phone
Alabama	revenue.alabama.gov	334-242-1170
Alaska	www.revenue.state.ak.us	907-269-6620
Arizona	www.azdor.gov	800-352-4090
Arkansas	www.dfa.arkansas.gov/offices/incomeTax/individual/Pages/default.aspx	501-682-1100
California	www.ftb.ca.gov/index.shtml?disabled=true	800-852-5711
Colorado	www.colorado.gov/revenue	303-238-7378
Connecticut	www.ct.gov/drs/site/default.asp	860-297-5962
Delaware	revenue.delaware.gov	302-577-8200
District of Columbia	otr.cfo.dc.gov/otr/site/default.asp	202-727-4829
Florida	dor.myflorida.com/dor	800-352-3671
Georgia	etax.dor.ga.gov	877-423-6711
Hawaii	www.state.hi.us/tax/tax.html	800-222-3229
Idaho	tax.idaho.gov	800-972-7660

Illinois	www.revenue.state.il.us/#t=tab1	800-732-8866
Indiana	www.in.gov/dor	317-232-2240
Iowa	www.iowa.gov/tax	800-367-3388
Kansas	ksrevenue.org	785-368-8222
Kentucky	revenue.ky.gov	502-564-4581
Louisiana	www.rev.state.la.us	225-219-0102
Maine	www.maine.gov/revenue	207-626-8475
Maryland	individuals.marylandtaxes.com	800-638-2937
Massachusetts	www.mass.gov/dor	800-392-6089
Michigan	www.michigan.gov/taxes/0,4676,7-238-44143-268091-- ,00.html	517-636-4486
Minnesota	www.revenue.state.mn.us/Pages/default.aspx	800-652-9094
Mississippi	www.dor.ms.gov	601-923-7000
Missouri	dor.mo.gov	573-751-3505
Montana	revenue.mt.gov/default.mcpx	866-859-2254
Nebraska	www.revenue.state.ne.us	800-742-7474
Nevada	tax.state.nv.us	866-962-3707
New Hampshire	www.revenue.nh.gov	603-230-5000
New Jersey	www.state.nj.us/treasury/revenue	800-323-4400
New Mexico	www.tax.newmexico.gov/Pages/TRD-Homepage.aspx	505-827-0700
New York	www.tax.ny.gov	518-457-5181
North Carolina	www.dor.state.nc.us	877-252-3052
North Dakota	www.nd.gov/tax	701-328-7088
Ohio	www.tax.ohio.gov	800-282-1780
Oklahoma	www.oktax.state.ok.us	405-521-3160
Oregon	www.oregon.gov/DOR	503-378-4988
Pennsylvania	www.revenue.state.pa.us/portal/server.pt/community/revenue_home/10648	717-787-8201
Rhode Island	www.tax.state.ri.us	401-574-8829

South Carolina	www.sctax.org/default.htm	803-898-5709
South Dakota	www.state.sd.us/drr2/Revenue.html	800-829-9188
Tennessee	www.state.tn.us/revenue	800-342-1003
Texas	www.window.state.tx.us	800-252-1389
Utah	tax.utah.gov	800-662-4335
Vermont	www.state.vt.us/tax/index.shtml	802-828-2865
Virginia	www.tax.virginia.gov	804-367-8031
Washington	dor.wa.gov/Content/Home/Default.aspx	800-647-7706
West Virginia	www.revenue.wv.gov/Pages/default.aspx	800-982-8297
Wisconsin	www.dor.state.wi.us	608-266-2486
Wyoming	revenue.state.wy.us	307-777-7961

Where to File Your US Individual Income Tax Return (Form 1040)

Note: The following locations may change from time to time. Double check before sending returns to these addresses.

Location	If you *are* not enclosing a payment, send to the following address.	If you *are* enclosing a payment, send to the following address.
Alabama, Georgia, North Carolina, or South Carolina	Department of the Treasury Internal Revenue Service Kansas City, MO 64999-0002	Internal Revenue Service PO Box 105017 Atlanta, GA 30348-5017
Florida, Louisiana, Mississippi, or Texas	Department of the Treasury Internal Revenue Service Austin, TX 73301-0002	Internal Revenue Service PO Box 1214 Charlotte, NC 28201-1214

Alaska, Arizona, California, Colorado, Hawaii, Nevada, Oregon, or Washington	Department of the Treasury Internal Revenue Service Fresno, CA 93888-0002	Internal Revenue Service PO Box 7704 San Francisco, CA 94120-7704
Arkansas, Idaho, Illinois, Indiana, Iowa, Kansas, Michigan, Minnesota, Montana, Nebraska, New Mexico, North Dakota, Ohio, Oklahoma, South Dakota, Utah, Wisconsin, or Wyoming	Department of the Treasury Internal Revenue Service Fresno, CA 93888-0002	Internal Revenue Service PO Box 802501 Cincinnati, OH 45280-2501
Kentucky, Missouri, New Jersey, Tennessee, Virginia, or West Virginia	Department of the Treasury Internal Revenue Service Kansas City, MO 84999-0002	Internal Revenue Service PO. 970011 St. Louis, MO 63197-0011
Connecticut, Delaware, District of Columbia, Maine, Maryland, Massachusetts, New Hampshire, New York, Pennsylvania, Rhode Island, or Vermont	Department of the Treasury Internal Revenue Service Kansas City, MO 84999-0002	Internal Revenue Service PO 37008 Hartford, CT 06176-0008

About the Authors

Dale A. Walters, CPA, PFS, CFP® (U.S. and Canada)
Partner and CEO, KeatsConnelly

Since he was young, Dale Walters has had a passion for helping others. He considered both traditionally helpful fields of law and medicine, but his natural talent for numbers led him into accounting, an industry that helps people with some of the hardest decisions in their lives: financial decisions.

He has been helping people with their financial decisions since 1980. Along the way, Dale earned the U.S. and Canadian Certified Financial Planner™ (CFP®) designations, the Certified Public Accountant (CPA) license, and the Personal Financial Specialist (PFS) designation. Early in his career, Dale spent some time in the tax department of the "Big Four" accounting firm of KPMG, but since 1994 he has been with KeatsConnelly, where he is now the Chief Executive Officer.

Dale considers his life a series of fortunate events, beginning with getting involved in high school sports, specifically wrestling. Sports provide enough motivation and structure to keep him out of the many troubles that await a teenager growing up in the projects. Wrestling lead to other fortunate events such as getting involved in Judo, where eventually became a fourth-degree black belt. Wrestling also lead to Walters receiving a wrestling scholarship to Drake University where he met his wife of over 30 years, the very first weekend of school.

Even the fact that Dale works at KeatsConnelly came about because of a chance meeting with Bob Keats and Tom Connelly. The three of us met at a professional education meeting, after a brief introduction we agreed to get together for lunch to discuss possibly referring business to each other; I was working at a small accounting firm at the time. We met but nothing came of it until they called Dale about six months later to ask him if he wanted to come to work for them.

In keeping with the fortunate events in his life, working at KeatsConnelly has afforded Dale a mentor in Bob Keats. In addition to being a dual citizen of the United States and Canada, and one of the top cross-border advisors, Keats is also the author of *The Border Guide*, a Canadian best-selling book focused on living, working, investing and retiring on both sides of the border. Armed with his mentor, Dale earned his Canadian CFP designation, making him one of the very first people to hold the designation on both sides of the border; Bob Keats is believed to be the first to do so.

Since becoming the CEO in 2004, Dale has led the firm to a number of prestigious awards for ethics, community volunteerism, workplace flexibility, and company culture, all of which led to KeatsConnelly being named one of Arizona's Most Admired Companies in 2011. The firm has also been named a top CPA financial planning firm in the nation by CPA Wealth Provider magazine on more than one occasion. Today, the company has over 35 employees and offices in Phoenix, Arizona, Boynton Beach, Florida, and Calgary, Alberta.

On the personal side, Dale has a passion for martial arts. Besides wrestling in college, Dale competed successfully in Judo having placed in the top five, four times, in the U.S. Junior National Championships (age 19 and under) and is now a fourth-degree black belt in Judo.

Another fortunate event is when Dale moved to Phoenix looking for a place to practice his Judo; he called a number in the Yellow Pages that offered Judo and Karate. As it turned out, the instructor was Robert Trias, 10th degree black belt (Grand Master) in Karate and founder of Karate in the U.S. Through Mr. Trias' instruction, Dale went on to become a four-time world heavyweight karate champion. Dale retired from competition in 1989, but continued to teach judo until he focused all of his energies as CEO of KeatsConnelly in 2004.

With the writing of this book, Dale continues to help others by helping the readers of this book avoid the potential tax mistakes of Canadians living in the U.S.

Sally Taylor, CPA, PFS, CFP® (US), MSFP
Partner and Director of Financial Planning, KeatsConnelly

Sally Taylor is the Director of Financial Planning, a Senior Planner, and a partner at Keats-
-Connelly. Sally has the responsibility for supervising the financial planning department and financial planning process at KeatsConnelly, as well as serving as the firm's financial planning committee chair. Sally works with the firm's clients to create plans that allow them to live a cross-border lifestyle. A cross border plan includes tax planning and preparation, estate planning, retirement planning, immigration and health care, as well as investment planning. She has been active in the wealth management since 1994, when she worked with one of the first multi-family offices in the United States, at that time. She has held senior positions with Sterling Ltd., National City Bank, and Clanco Management Corporation. She was instrumental in developing the service model that allowed her previous firm to grow from $200 million under management to nearly $1 billion in three years. She has an extensive background in alternative assets, tax planning and estate planning, and most recently has added cross-border Canadian/US tax and financial planning to her wide-ranging areas of expertise. Sally has worked with KeatsConnelly since 2007 when she and her husband Ed, moved from Cleveland, Ohio to Phoenix.

She graduated with a BS in Accountancy from John Carroll University, a Jesuit University located in University Heights, Ohio. She is a Certified Public Accountant (CPA) and has a Masters of Financial Planning from the College for Financial Planning in Denver, Colorado. She is also a Personal Financial Specialist (PFS) and a Certified Financial Planner™ (CFP®) professional in the United States.

Sally is active in many organizations including Soroptimist International of Phoenix, Vistage, the Central Arizona Estate Planning Council, the Arizona Society of CPAs, the American Institute of CPAs, the Financial Planning Association, and Toastmasters International. Sally is a frequent speaker on topics that include Canadians owning real estate in the U.S., cross-border retirement planning, and tax and immigration planning for Canadians.

Sally and her husband live in Mesa, Arizona with their rescued greyhound and three cats.

David Levine, CA, CPA
Partner and International Tax Manager, KeatsConnelly

David Levine is a partner and the International Tax Manager at KeatsConnelly, the largest and most experienced cross-border wealth management firm in North America that specializes in assisting Canadians and Americans realize their dreams of a cross-border lifestyle. David holds Bachelor of Science and Bachelor of Commerce (Honors Business Administration) degrees. David is a Chartered Accountant (Ontario) and a Certified Public Accountant (Florida) and has practiced in the cross border tax area for more than 25 years. David has been quoted by the Canadian Press and the Sun Sentinel. David joined KeatsConnelly in 2005 and was responsible for helping the firm open the Florida office that year. David continues to live in Florida with his wife Shelley.